ARMOURED FIGHTING VEHICLES

OF THE WORLD

ARMOURED
FIGHTING
VEHICLES
OF THE WORLD

General Editor: Peter Darman

This edition published in 2004 by Grange Books
Grange Books plc
The Grange
1–6 Kingsnorth Estate
Hoo
Near Rochester
Kent ME3 9ND
www.grangebooks.co.uk

© 2004 The Brown Reference Group plc

ISBN 1-84013-680-4

Printed in China

Editorial and design:
The Brown Reference Group plc
8 Chapel Place
Rivington Street
London
EC2A 3DQ
UK
www.brownreference.com

ARMOURED
FIGHTING
VEHICLES

CONTENTS

ARMOURED
SUPPORT AND
ENGINEER
VEHICLES

CONTENTS

SK 105

Steyr-Daimler-Puch Spezialfahrzeug AG & Co KG developed the SK 105 light tank, known as the *Kurassier*, to meet the Austrian Army's operational requirement for a mobile anti-tank vehicle. Although classified as "tank destroyer" (*Jagdpanzer*) by the Austrian Army, it is considered a light tank. The first pre-production vehicles were completed in 1971, and since then almost 700 have been built for home and export markets. The SK 105 shares many common automotive components with the Steyr fully tracked armoured personnel carrier. It is fitted with a two-man oscillating turret armed with a 105mm rifled gun, which is fed by two revolver-type magazines, each of which holds six rounds. The empty cartridge cases are ejected outside of the turret bustle at the rear. The SK 105 has been constantly improved, and the latest production version features a computerized fire control system with day/night sights for the commander and gunner and a new fully automatic transmission. Options for the SK 105 include an upgrade package to bring older vehicles up to the latest production standard, NBC (nuclear, biological, chemical) protection system and new night-vision equipment. Many of its automotive components are identical to those used in the armoured troop carrier vehicles built by Steyr.

SPECIFICATIONS

Type:	*light tank*
Crew:	*3*
Weight:	*17,500kg (38,500lb)*
Length (Gun Forward):	*7.76m (25.45ft)*
Height:	*2.88m (9.44ft)*
Width:	*2.5m (8.2ft)*
Ground Clearance:	*0.4m (1.3ft)*
Vertical Obstacle:	*0.8m (2.62ft)*
Trench:	*2.4m (7.87ft)*
Gradient:	*75 percent*
Powerplant:	*Steyr 7FA diesel*
Power Rating:	*320hp*
Speed – Maximum:	*68km/h (42.5mph)*
Cruising Range:	*520km (325 miles)*
Main Armament:	*1 x 105mm*
Secondary Armament:	*2 x 7.62mm*
Ammunition:	*41 x 105mm, 2000 x 7.62mm*

TYPE 85

The Type 85 tank is a modification of the earlier Type 80, which was in turn based on the Soviet T-54, with an improved turret changed from a cast design to a welded variant. The newest model, the Type 85-III, incorporates features also found in the newer Type 90 tank, including a larger 125mm smoothbore main gun capable of firing armour-piercing, fin-stabilized, discarding sabot (APFSDS), high-explosive, anti-tank (HEAT) and high-explosive, anti-tank fragmentation (HEAT-FRAG) rounds. The more recent BK-27 HEAT round offers increased penetration against conventional armour and explosive reactive armour (ERA). The BK-29 round, with a hard penetrator in the nose, is designed for use against reactive armour and also has fragmentation effects. A stabilized image intensification sight allows the Type 85 to engage moving targets while in motion. A GEC-Marconi Centaur fire control system is also available, while the British Barr and Stroud thermal-based fire control system can be fitted. The Type 85-III uses modular composite armour, and some reports suggest the incorporation of reactive armour. Composite panels are available to improve protection, while the crew can achieve a rate of fire of up to six rounds per minute, though it is customary for crews to halt before firing.

SPECIFICATIONS

Type:	main battle tank
Crew:	3
Weight:	41,000kg (90,200lb)
Length (Gun Forward):	10.28m (33.72ft)
Height:	2.3m (7.54ft)
Width:	3.45m (11.31ft)
Ground Clearance:	0.48m (1.57ft)
Vertical Obstacle:	0.8m (2.62ft)
Trench:	2.7m (8.85ft)
Gradient:	60 percent
Powerplant:	V-12 supercharged diesel
Power Rating:	730hp
Speed – Maximum:	57.25km/h (35.78mph)
Cruising Range:	500km (312 miles)
Main Armament:	1 x 125mm
Secondary Armament:	1 x 7.62mm , 1 x 12.7mm
Ammunition:	40 x 125mm, 2000 x 7.62mm

TYPE 90

The Type 90 incorporates significant improvements over the Type 85, including modular composite armour, a stabilized turret, slaved targeting sight and gun, passive thermal imaging, and an autoloading, smoothbore 125mm gun capable of firing armour-piercing, fin-stabilized, discarding sabot (APFSDS), high-explosive, anti-tank (HEAT) and high-explosive, anti-tank fragmentation (HEAT-FRAG) rounds. A family of explosive reactive armour (ERA) systems has been developed by China North Industries Corporation (NORINCO). The armour improves survivability against high-explosive, anti-tank (HEAT), kinetic energy and tandem HEAT projectiles. With the addition of reactive armour panels, an improved laser rangefinder and increased mobility, the Type 90-II is currently the most advanced Chinese main battle tank. Although not yet in service in large quantities, it is known that the People's Liberation Army (PLA) ordered 00 Type 90-IIs, without advanced fire control systems, in 1999. China, following Russian tradition, has mounted anti-tank guided weapons on its tanks, and the latest is the Red Arrow 9 anti-tank guided weapon (ATGW). The Type 90 should enter service in large numbers, but given the fragile state of China's finances, it is not known how many Type 90s will ultimately be built.

SPECIFICATIONS

Type:	main battle tank
Crew:	3
Weight:	43,636kg (96,000lb)
Length (Gun Forward):	10.28m (33.72ft)
Height:	2.3m (7.54ft)
Width:	3.45m (11.31ft)
Ground Clearance:	0.48m (1.57ft)
Vertical Obstacle:	0.8m (2.62ft)
Trench:	2.7m (8.85ft)
Gradient:	60 percent
Powerplant:	8-cylinder turbocharged diesel
Power Rating:	1200hp
Speed – Maximum:	59km/h (37mph)
Cruising Range:	unknown
Main Armament:	1 x 125mm
Secondary Armament:	1 x 12.7mm, 1 x 7.62mm
Ammunition:	unknown

ADATS

ADATS (Air Defence Anti-Tank System) is one of the world's premier low-level air defence systems. It uses pulse-Doppler radar and electro-optics to detect targets and engage them with accurate laser beam-rider guided missiles. ADATS employs an integrated command, control and communications (C3) network that can coordinate the firepower of up to six ADATS systems. The ADATS system itself is highly mobile. For example, it can be mounted on a variety of mobile platforms such as the M113 and M3 Bradley vehicles. The system includes a fully automatic real-time data exchange with airspace control data, weapon control orders and fire control orders, target identification data, individual system status and vehicle position, threat prioritization and optimized weapon allocation. A six-unit ADATS network can engage up to 48 air or ground targets simultaneously. Initial target detection to missile launch takes less than five seconds. The tracker search and target acquisition sequence is carried out using the forward-looking infrared (FLIR) and the television sighting system. Missile launch and guidance uses FLIR and television target tracking and carbon dioxide laser beam-riding missile guidance. The time required to launch a second missile following completion of the first engagement is less than two seconds.

SPECIFICATIONS

Type:	self-propelled SAM
Crew:	3
Weight:	22,940kg (50,468lb)
Length:	6.55 m (21.48ft)
Height:	2.97m (9.74ft)
Width:	3.61m (11.84ft)
Ground Clearance:	0.43m (1.41ft)
Vertical Obstacle:	0.91m (2.98ft)
Trench:	2.54m (8.33ft)
Gradient:	60 percent
Powerplant:	VTA-903T turbocharged diesel
Power Rating:	500hp
Speed – Maximum:	60km/h (37.5mph)
Cruising Range:	483km (302 miles)
Main Armament:	8 ready-to-fire SAMs
Secondary Armament:	none
Ammunition:	8 x SAM

CV 90

The Combat Vehicle 90 (CV 90) is jointly developed and manufactured by Hägglunds AB (chassis) and Bofors AB (turret, armament and ammunition). The CV 90 family consists of a number of variants: CV 90 (the basic armoured infantry fighting vehicle, armed with a 30mm automatic cannon); anti-aircraft vehicle 90; forward observer vehicle 90; command post vehicle 90; and recovery vehicle 90. All are designed for use in inhospitable terrain and hostile combat environments. The CV 90 is an extremely agile, multirole combat vehicle with all-target capability, a low, very compact structure and minimized radar and infrared signatures. The basic turret is electrically operated and houses a sight with integrated laser rangefinder and thermal camera. The 30mm cannon can knock out all other light armoured vehicles and even offers a chance to kill enemy tanks from flanking positions. A total of 500 CV 90s have been procured for the Swedish Army, with final delivery taking place in 2002. The Hägglunds Vehicle CV 90120 light tank consists of a slightly modified CV 90 chassis, produced for both Norway and Sweden, and fitted with a new three-man turret mounting a Swiss Ordnance 120mm smoothbore gun with a computerized fire control system and stabilized day/night sights.

SPECIFICATIONS

Type:	infantry fighting vehicle
Crew:	3 + 8
Weight:	26,000kg (57,200lb)
Length:	6.54m (21.45ft)
Height:	2.73m (8.95ft)
Width:	3.19m (10.46ft)
Ground Clearance:	0.45m (1.47ft)
Vertical Obstacle:	1.2m (3.93ft)
Trench:	2.4m (7.87ft)
Gradient:	60 percent
Powerplant:	Scania DSI 14 diesel
Power Rating:	605hp
Speed – Maximum:	70km/h (43.75mph)
Cruising Range:	unknown
Main Armament:	1 x 30mm
Secondary Armament:	1 x 7.62mm
Ammunition:	400 x 30mm, 3800 x 7.62mm

TAM

The TAM (*Tanque Argentino Mediano* – Argentine Medium Tank) is a military vehicle based on the German Marder 1 infantry vehicle. The main differences include different powerpacks and slightly heavier armour for the tank version. The TAM and the infantry version, the VCTP (*Vehículo de Combate Transporte de Personal* – Combat Vehicle Personnel Transport), were shown as prototypes in the mid-1970s and are now the standard equipment of Argentine Army mechanized units. A family of derivative vehicles in various stages of development include the VCPM mortar carrier, VCRC recovery vehicle, VCTC command vehicle, VCLC rocket launcher, and a self-propelled howitzer carrying a locally produced version of the Italian Palmaria gun. The first few TAMs were equipped with the locally produced variant of the L7A1 gun. Later vehicles were armed with the Rheinmetall LTA2, and the last produced vehicles were equipped with a locally produced modified version of the French CN-105-57, produced in the TAMSE military factory of Rio Tercero, in Cordoba province. The TAM is also equipped with two smoke grenade launchers, with each launcher firing four grenades. In addition, the vehicle is NBC proof and can be fitted with a night-vision system.

SPECIFICATIONS

Type:	medium tank
Crew:	4
Weight:	30,000kg (66,000lb)
Length (Gun Forward):	8.23m (27ft)
Height:	2.43m (7.97ft)
Width:	3.29m (10.79ft)
Ground Clearance:	0.45m (1.47ft)
Vertical Obstacle:	1m (3.28ft)
Trench:	2.5m (8.2ft)
Gradient:	60 percent
Powerplant:	MTU MB 833 Ka 500 diesel
Power Rating:	720hp
Speed – Maximum:	75km/h (46.87mph)
Cruising Range:	550km (344 miles)
Main Armament:	1 x 105mm
Secondary Armament:	1 x 7.62mm
Ammunition:	50 x 105mm, 6000 x 7.62mm

AMX-10P

The AMX-10P is the support and freight vehicle of the mechanized infantry units, and it carries squadrons of the combat regiments. This tracked amphibious armoured vehicle transports a group of nine men in addition to the driver and gunner under the turret. It has a great autonomy and excellent terrestrial and water mobility which allows it, in particular, to cross by its own means a flooded cut. Its 20mm gun enables it to engage light armoured tanks and even low-flying aircraft. Protected against weapons of average gauge and the shrapnel of artillery shells, it can also fight in an NBC environment. A French SNPE explosive reactive armour (ERA) kit is available for use on the AMX-10P. However, during combat ERA would be a hazard to dismounting troops and so passive armour is preferable. There are a number of variants of this vehicle: the basic AMX-10P with Milan or HOT anti-tank guided missiles (ATGMs) AMX-10P/Milan; AMX-10 PAC 90, a fire support/anti-tank variant with a Giat 90mm gun; AMX-10P Marine, an improved amphibious variant with a 12.7mm, 25mm or 90mm gun; AMX-10 PC, a command variant with varied command stations; AMX-10 RC, a wheeled (6 x 6) fire support vehicle armed with a 90mm gun; and AMX-10 RAC, the same fire support chassis with a 105mm gun.

SPECIFICATIONS

Type:	infantry combat vehicle
Crew:	2 + 9
Weight:	14,500kg (31,900lb)
Length:	5.75m (18.86ft)
Height:	2.57m (8.43ft)
Width:	2.78m (9.12ft)
Ground Clearance:	0.45m (1.47ft)
Vertical Obstacle:	0.7m (2.2ft)
Trench:	2.1m (6.88ft)
Gradient:	60 percent
Powerplant:	Scania DSI 14 diesel
Power Rating:	300hp
Speed – Maximum:	70km/h (43.75mph)
Cruising Range:	600km (375 miles)
Main Armament:	1 x 20mm
Secondary Armament:	1 x 7.62mm
Ammunition:	800 x 20mm, 2000 x 7.62mm

AMX-13

esign work on the AMX-13 light tank began in 1946 at the Atelier de Construction d'Issy-les-Moulineaux and the first prototype was completed two years later. Production was undertaken at the Atelier de Construction Roanne (ARE) from 1952, with the first production tanks completed the following year. At one time production of the tank was running at 45 units per month but in the early 1960s production of the whole family was transferred to the civilian company of Creusot-Loire at Chalon sur Saône as the ARE was tooling up for production of the AMX-30. The basic AMX-13 chassis has been used for a wide range of vehicles, including self-propelled guns and anti-aircraft systems. Improvements include a new power-pack consisting of a diesel engine coupled to a fully automatic transmission and the replacement of the torsion bar suspension by a new hydropneumatic suspension for improved cross-country mobility. The AMX-13 is no longer being marketed by Giat Industries. It is estimated that total production of the AMX-13 family of light tracked vehicles, including the light tank, amounted to 7700 units, of which around 3400 were exported. The AMX-13 tank was phased out of service with the French Army many years ago, but it is still in use in the developing world.

SPECIFICATIONS

Type:	light tank
Crew:	3
Weight:	15,000kg (33,000lb)
Length (Gun Forward):	6.36m (20.86ft)
Height:	2.3m (7.54ft)
Width:	2.51m (8.23ft)
Ground Clearance:	0.3/m (1.21ft)
Vertical Obstacle:	0.65m (2.13ft)
Trench:	1.6m (5.24ft)
Gradient:	60 percent
Powerplant:	SOFAM Model 8 petrol
Power Rating:	250hp
Speed – Maximum:	60km/h (37.5mph)
Cruising Range:	400km (250 miles)
Main Armament:	1 x 90mm
Secondary Armament:	2 x 7.62mm
Ammunition:	32 x 90mm, 3600 x 7.62mm

AMX-30

Giat Industries has built and delivered to a dozen armies almost 2300 AMX-30 main battle tanks, as well as 1100 derivative versions (155 GCT self-propelled howitzers, anti-aircraft missile or gun systems and armoured recovery vehicles). The AMX-30 B2 is an improved version of the tank, achieved either by rebuilding existing models or by production of new tanks, and is equipped with an automatic fire control system. The AMX-30 is well profiled, strongly armed, equipped with very good mobility and a great autonomy. It is encased in rolled plates and castings, entirely welded and has a cast turret. Its lack of composite armour puts it at a distinct disadvantage in tank-versus-tank engagements. In reality, it is protected only from small-gauge weapons and the effects of artillery. The AMX-30 B2 is able to fight in an NBC environment and to cross water up to 2m (6.5ft) deep (4m [13.12ft] with a snorkel). It is intended for all missions requiring operations by traditional armoured forces: the direct destruction of the enemy forces, and the immediate exploitation of break-throughs achieved by other weapon systems, including the battlefield deployment of nuclear weapons. The AMX-30 is now no longer in French frontline service, having been replaced by the Leclerc.

SPECIFICATIONS

Type:	main battle tank
Crew:	4
Weight:	36,000kg (79,200lb)
Length (Gun Forward):	9.48m (31.1ft)
Height:	2.85m (9.35ft)
Width:	3.1m (10.17ft)
Ground Clearance:	0.44m (1.44ft)
Vertical Obstacle:	0.93m (3.05ft)
Trench:	2.9m (9.51ft)
Gradient:	60 percent
Powerplant:	Hispano-Suiza HS 110
Power Rating:	720hp
Speed – Maximum:	65km/h (40.62mph)
Cruising Range:	600km (375 miles)
Main Armament:	1 x 105mm
Secondary Armament:	1 x 20mm, 1 x 7.62mm
Ammunition:	47 x 105mm, 1050 x 20mm

AUF-1

This 155mm self-propelled howitzer is intended to equip forces with armoured artillery to provide direct and indirect fire. The 155mm gun is assembled from a turret on the chassis of the AMX-30, providing mobility close to that of the main battle tank. The gun's range is 23.5km (14.68 miles) with normal ammunition and 30km (18.75 miles) with long-range ammunition. Normal ammunition is a high-explosive shell with a hollow base. The initial speed in maximum loading is 810 metres pre second (2657 feet per second). The vehicle is capable of carrying 42 complete rounds: 7 racks of 6 shells, 7 racks of 6 combustible casings. Re-stocking of ammunition can be achieved in 15 minutes with 4 men. The pace of firing with an automatic attachment feeding in ammunition, using combustible casings, allows the gun to fire 6 shots in 45 seconds and 12 shots in 2 minutes. In the event of a partial or total breakdown of this device, firing is still possible manually but at reduced rate. The vehicle can operate on an NBC battlefield due to the sealing of the turret, and the crew is also protected from the projectiles of light automatic weapons. The secondary armament is a 12.7mm machine gun, which provides some defence against aircraft and enemy infantry. The AUF-1 was used by Coalition forces in the 1991 Gulf War.

SPECIFICATIONS

Type:	self-propelled howitzer
Crew:	4
Weight:	42,000kg (92,400lb)
Length (Gun Forward):	10.25m (33.62ft)
Height:	3.25m (10.66ft)
Width:	3.15m (10.33ft)
Ground Clearance:	0.42m (1.37ft)
Vertical Obstacle:	0.93m (3.05ft)
Trench:	1.9m (6.23ft)
Gradient:	60 percent
Powerplant:	Hispano-Suiza HS 110
Power Rating:	720hp
Speed – Maximum:	60km/h (37.5mph)
Cruising Range:	450km (281 miles)
Main Armament:	1 x 155mm
Secondary Armament:	1 x 12.7mm
Ammunition:	42 x 155mm, 800 x 12.7mm

CROTALE

rotale is an all-weather, short-range air defence system whose mission is the defence of frontline
armoured brigades, permanent or semi-permanent
site defence, and area defence against air threats: fixed-wing
aircraft, attack helicopters, cruise missiles, tactical missiles
and saturation attacks with stand-off weapons released from
aircraft and helicopters. The Crotale system provides air
situation and threat assessment, extended detection range,
identification friend-or-foe (IFF), multi-target detection plus
automated acquisition, and tracking and engagement. The
latest version Crotale Next Generation (NG) entered production in 1990 and is in service with the Finnish Army (20
systems), the French Air Force (12 shelter-mounted systems) and the French Navy. The manufacturer, Thales
Optronics, signed a contract with Greece in June 1999 for
11 Crotale NG systems: nine for the Air Force and two for
the Navy. It has also been sold to Saudi Arabia and Oman.
The system is equipped with a multi-sensor suite including
passive electro-optics and radar with built-in electronic
counter countermeasures (ECCM) to engage airborne targets under adverse conditions of dense electronic warfare
and hostile battlefield environments, including NBC and
smoke and dust screens.

SPECIFICATIONS

Type:	self-propelled SAM
Crew:	3
Weight:	18,182kg (40,000lb)
Length:	4.86m (16ft)
Height:	2.68m (8.79ft)
Width:	2.68m (8.79ft)
Ground Clearance:	0.43m (1.41ft)
Vertical Obstacle:	0.61m (2ft)
Trench:	2.18m (7.15ft)
Gradient:	60 percent
Powerplant:	Detroit Diesel 6V53TIA
Power Rating:	400hp
Speed – Maximum:	66km/h (41mph)
Cruising Range:	480km (300 miles)
Main Armament:	8 x Crotale NG VT1 missiles
Secondary Armament:	none
Ammunition:	Crotale NG VT1 missiles

LECLERC

The Leclerc was designed to be highly capable in combat against all potential enemy tanks in day or night at ranges in excess of 3000m (9842ft). It includes a gun with an automatic loading system which makes it possible to quickly select the type of ammunition, and is capable of firing when the tank is moving and can achieve a rate of fire of up to six shots per minute. The long-range fire control system stabilizes the sight, keeping the gun permanently pointed at the target. There are two sights: one for the commander of the tank and the other for the operator. The turret acquires the target with gyro-stabilizers, and a video re-copy of the images allows sharing of information between the two. Unequalled mobility is obtained by the synergy between the motor, the kinematic chain, and the hydropneumatic suspension. A very balanced general protection is obtained not only by modular shieldings but also by compactness and thus low visibility, which, combined with the very great agility of the tank, makes it a difficult target to hit. Onboard, tactical or logistic decisions are made easier by the digitalization of all data. The radio operator station makes it possible to coordinate the whole of the armoured battle group by the use of the system of control and command installed on board the Leclerc.

SPECIFICATIONS

Type:	main battle tank
Crew:	3
Weight:	54,500kg (119,900lb)
Length (Gun Forward):	9.87m (32.38ft)
Height:	2.53m (8.3ft)
Width:	3.71m (12.17ft)
Ground Clearance:	0.5m (1.64ft)
Vertical Obstacle:	1.25m (4.1ft)
Trench:	3m (9.84ft)
Gradient:	60 percent
Powerplant:	SACM V8X diesel
Power Rating:	1500hp
Speed – Maximum:	71km/h (44.3mph)
Cruising Range:	550km (344 miles)
Main Armament:	1 x 120mm
Secondary Armament:	2 x 12.7mm
Ammunition:	40 x 120mm

ROLAND 2

The Roland 2 weapon system is intended for the anti-aircraft defence of armoured and mechanized units to counter aircraft flying to nearly Mach 1.5 and hovering helicopters. Roland is generally employed either in complement of the coverage of the American Hawk system's defence of zones and corridors not defended by the latter, or as an extension of the Hawk system itself. The Hawk missile is a surface-to-air missile (SAM) system that provides medium-range air defence against both aircraft and missiles. Roland ensures the overall defence of a zone of 100 square kilometres (62.5 square miles) against a threat posed by a flight of four aircraft or two flights acting at more than 20-second intervals. Deployed on a tracked vehicle derived from the AMX-30 main battle tank, it comprises a radar with a range of 16km (10 miles), a sighting tube with an infrared locator that measures the difference between the missile in flight and the line of sight of the fire control radar, and a computer antenna for remote control. The target is detected by the radar, and the continuation of the target after acquisition is carried out manually in radar mode. Roland has a reload time of around 10 seconds, though this may increase in a battlefield environment. The missiles themselves have an altitude of 5500m (16,404ft).

SPECIFICATIONS

Type:	self-propelled SAM
Crew:	3
Weight:	32,500kg (71,500kg)
Length:	6.91m (22.67ft)
Height:	2.92m (9.58ft)
Width:	3.24m (10.62ft)
Ground Clearance:	0.44m (1.44ft)
Vertical Obstacle:	1.15m (3.72ft)
Trench:	2.5m (8.2ft)
Gradient:	60 percent
Powerplant:	MTU MB 833 Ea 500 diesel
Power Rating:	600hp
Speed – Maximum:	70km/h (43.75mph)
Cruising Range:	520km (325 miles)
Main Armament:	2 x Roland SAM
Secondary Armament:	1 x 7.62mm
Ammunition:	8 x Roland SAM

ASRAD

The light mechanized Short-Range Air Defence System (SHORAD) has been developed for the German Army by STN ATLAS Elektronik GmbH in Bremen and Krauss-Maffei Wegmann (KMW) in Kassel, Germany. The export version is known as the Atlas Short-Range Air Defence System (ASRAD). It is based on the Wiesel 2 carrier vehicle and provides protection for vital assets such as command, control, communications and information centres (C3I centres), airfields and troops on the move, or on the battlefield against the threat of low-level fixed-wing and rotary wing aircraft. ASRAD carries four ready-to-fire surface-to-air missiles (SAMs), including the Stinger, Igla, the RBS 70 Mk 2 and others. It is air transportable in a CH-53 helicopter. Target acquisition is achieved either by the 3-D HARD radar installed on the platoon command post, which downloads target data via radio data link to the vehicle, or by the Pilkington Optronics Air Defence Alerting Device (ADAD) passive infrared search and track system (IRST), mounted on the forward part of the roof. For target tracking, the vehicle is equipped with its own stabilized forward-looking infrared (FLIR) sensor, TV and laser rangefinder as well as dual mode auto-tracking. The vehicle is lightweight, making it ideal for use with rapid-reaction and airborne forces.

SPECIFICATIONS

Type:	*self-propelled SAM*
Crew:	*3*
Weight:	*2800kg (6160kg)*
Length:	*3.31m (10.85ft)*
Height:	*2m (6.56ft)*
Width:	*1.82m (5.97ft)*
Ground Clearance:	*0.3m (0.98ft)*
Vertical Obstacle:	*0.4m (1.13ft)*
Trench:	*1.2m (3.93ft)*
Gradient:	*60 percent*
Powerplant:	*VW turbocharged diesel*
Power Rating:	*86hp*
Speed – Maximum:	*75km/h (46.87mph)*
Cruising Range:	*300km (188 miles)*
Main Armament:	*4 x SAM*
Secondary Armament:	*none*
Ammunition:	*unknown*

GEPARD

The vehicle is fitted with a fire control system, all-weather tracking, acquisition sensors and powerful automatic guns. Its role is to protect key installations, combat units and troops on the move and on the battlefield. Gepard is fitted with a two-man electric-operated turret armed with twin Oerlikon KDA 35mm guns, which have automatic belt feed. The rate of fire provided by the two barrels is 1100 rounds per minute, and each gun has 320 rounds of ready-to-fire anti-air ammunition and 20 rounds of anti-ground target ammunition. The guns are capable of firing a range of standardized 35mm ammunition including the latest frangible armour-piercing, discarding sabot (FAPDS) round, which has a muzzle velocity over 1400 mps (4593fps). The Gepard is equipped with eight smoke dischargers installed on either side of the turret for protection, and future plans include fitting the Stinger surface-to-air missile (SAM) system, whose launching system will be fitted on the side of the 35mm twin guns. Gepard is equipped with independent search and tracking radars, the search radar installed at the front rear of the turret and the tracking radar on the rear front of the turret. The radars provide 360-degree scanning with simultaneous target tracking, clutter suppression and search-on-the-move capability.

SPECIFICATIONS

Type:	self-propelled anti-aircraft gun
Crew:	3
Weight:	47,300kg (104,060lb)
Length (Gun Forward):	7.73m (25.36ft)
Height:	4.03m (13.22ft)
Width:	3.71m (12.17ft)
Ground Clearance:	0.5m (1.64ft)
Vertical Obstacle:	1.15m (3.77ft)
Trench:	3m (9.84ft)
Gradient:	60 percent
Powerplant:	Type OM314 diesel
Power Rating:	830hp
Speed – Maximum:	65km/h (40.62mph)
Cruising Range:	550km (344 miles)
Main Armament:	2 x 35mm
Secondary Armament:	none
Ammunition:	320 (AA) & 20 (AP) per gun

JAGUAR

The *Jagdpanzer Rakete* was a modern tank destroyer and featured the SS-11 missile. There were 370 built in 1967–68, and they shared the same chassis with the now-defunct *Jagdpanzer Kanone* 90mm self-propelled anti-tank gun. Between 1978 and 1983 316 of the original *Raketen* were rebuilt and their missiles upgraded to the more advanced Euromissile K3S ATGW. The armour on the front and sides was upgraded with appliqué packages to improve protection against HEAT warheads. These rebuilt vehicles were designated Jaguar 1s. Between 1983 and 1985, 162 vehicles were converted to the Jaguar 2, which fires tube-launched, optically tracked, wire guided (TOW) missiles. Prior to 1995, the tank destroyers were a separate branch in the army but are now integrated into the mechanized infantry as the 6th company of a panzergrenadier battalion. The Jaguar platoon consist of five vehicles (two sections of two plus the platoon leader). The vehicles have excellent optics. The main differences between the Jaguar 1 and 2 are different optics and a different loading mechanism for the TOW missiles. The Jaguar 2 has 12 TOW missiles with a reload time of approximately five seconds. Reloading is done automatically, and the vehicle remains sealed to allow the crew to fight in an NBC environment.

SPECIFICATIONS

Type:	anti-tank vehicle
Crew:	4
Weight:	25,500kg (56,100lb)
Length:	6.61m (21.68ft)
Height:	2.54m (8.33ft)
Width:	3.12m (10.23ft)
Ground Clearance:	0.45m (1.47ft)
Vertical Obstacle:	0.75m (2.46ft)
Trench:	2m (6.56ft)
Gradient:	58 percent
Powerplant:	Daimler-Benz MB 837 diesel
Power Rating:	500hp
Speed – Maximum:	70km/h (43.75mph)
Cruising Range:	400km (250 miles)
Main Armament:	1 x HOT ATGW launcher
Secondary Armament:	2 x 7.62mm
Ammunition:	12 x HOT, 3200 x 7.62mm

LEOPARD 1

The Leopard 1 was first produced in 1963 and more than 6000 vehicles have since been exported to nine NATO countries: Belgium, Denmark, Germany, Greece, Italy, Canada, the Netherlands, Norway and Turkey, and also Australia. The main gun can fire while on the move through the use of an electronic, hydraulic gyroscopic gun stabilizer. This is known as a fully stabilized power traverse. In addition, the Leopard is fitted with two banks of smoke grenade dischargers on the turret to create local smoke screens. The Leopard can be sealed against nuclear contamination on the battlefield. It is a minimum-maintenance armoured fighting vehicle with visual lubricant level checks and minimum crew maintenance required: complete engine replacement is possible in 30 minutes under field conditions. With preparation, it is capable of deep-fording or submerged fording where river banks are prepared for exit and entry. A number of countries are upgrading their Leopard 1s. The Belgians, for example, are modernizing their old Leopard 1 BE (delivered from 1968) with the new 1A5. In 1978 Norway took delivery of 78 Leopard 1s, and the Norwegian vehicles underwent a modernization programme that replaced the hydraulic gun control system by an all-electric system, bringing them up to A5 standard.

SPECIFICATIONS

Type:	*main battle tank*
Crew:	*4*
Weight:	*40,000kg (88,000lb)*
Length (Gun Forward):	*9.54kg (31.29ft)*
Height:	*2.61m (8.56ft)*
Width:	*3.37m (11.05ft)*
Ground Clearance:	*0.44m (1.44ft)*
Vertical Obstacle:	*1.15m (3.77ft)*
Trench:	*3m (9.84ft)*
Gradient:	*60 percent*
Powerplant:	*MTU MB 838 Ca M500*
Power Rating:	*830hp*
Speed – Maximum:	*65km/h (40.62mph)*
Cruising Range:	*600km (375 miles)*
Main Armament:	*1 x 105mm*
Secondary Armament:	*2 x 7.62mm*
Ammunition:	*60 x 105mm, 5500 x 7.62mm*

LEOPARD 2

The successor to the Leopard 1, the Leopard 2, was first produced in 1979. A variety of upgrade programmes and options are available for the Leopard 2, including the vehicle Integrated Command and Information System (IFIS), a digital command and information system. The Leopard 2 has had technical improvements under Upgrading Level I and Level II programmes. For example, a new smoothbore gun, the 120mm L55 gun, has been developed by Rheinmetall GmbH to replace the shorter 120mm L44 smoothbore gun. It permits effective use of the new APFSDS-T round – DM53 (LKE II) – which has a longer rod penetrator. The German Army has decided not to purchase the DM43 APFSDS-T round, but rather wait and upgrade to the DM53. Combat support variants of the Leopard 2 include an armoured recovery vehicle. The Leopard 2A5/Leopard 2 (Improved) is a recent upgrade with spaced armour added to turret front, and increased armour on the hull and side skirts. Other improvements include improved stabilization, suspension, navigation, fire control and hatch design. The Leopard 2E is a derivative of the A5 version, developed under a programme of co-manufacture between Spain and Germany. There is no doubt that the Leopard 2 is one of the finest main battle tanks in the world.

SPECIFICATIONS

Type:	main battle tank
Crew:	4
Weight:	62,000kg (136,400lb)
Length (Gun Forward):	9.97m (32.7ft)
Height:	3m (9.84ft)
Width:	3.74m (12.27ft)
Ground Clearance:	0.54m (1.77ft)
Vertical Obstacle:	1.1m (3.6ft)
Trench:	3m (9.84ft)
Gradient:	60 percent
Powerplant:	MTU MB 873 Ka 501
Power Rating:	1500hp
Speed – Maximum:	72km/h (45mph)
Cruising Range:	550km (344 miles)
Main Armament:	1 x 120mm
Secondary Armament:	2 x 7.62mm
Ammunition:	42 x 120mm, 4750 x 7.62mm

LEOPARD 2A6

The Leopard 2A6 is equipped with the L55 gun, an auxiliary engine, improved mine protection and an air-conditioning system. The hull is in three sections: the driving compartment at the front, the fighting section in the centre and the engine at the rear of the vehicle. The driver's compartment is equipped with three observation periscopes, and the space to the left of the driver is provided for ammunition stowage. A camera with a 65-degree horizontal and vertical field of view positioned at the rear of the vehicle and a television monitor provide a reversing aid for the driver. An upgrade programme provides third-generation composite armour, and the additional reinforcement to the turret frontal and lateral armour with externally mounted add-on armour modules. In the event of weapon penetration through the armour, the spall liner reduces the number of fragments and narrows the fragment cone. The reinforcement provides protection against multiple strike, kinetic energy rounds and shaped charges. A new smoothbore gun, the 120mm L55, replaces the shorter 120mm L44 smoothbore gun on the Leopard 2. The extension of the barrel length from calibre length 44 to calibre length 55 results in a greater portion of the available energy in the barrel being converted into projectile velocity.

SPECIFICATIONS

Type:	main battle tank
Crew:	4
Weight:	62,000kg (136,400lb)
Length (Gun Forward):	9.97m (32.7ft)
Height:	3m (9.84ft)
Width:	3.74m (12.27ft)
Ground Clearance:	0.54m (1.77ft)
Vertical Obstacle:	1.1m (3.6ft)
Trench:	3m (9.84ft)
Gradient:	60 percent
Powerplant:	MTU MB 873 Ka 501
Power Rating:	1500hp
Speed – Maximum:	72km/h (45mph)
Cruising Range:	500km (312 miles)
Main Armament:	1 x 120mm
Secondary Armament:	2 x 7.62mm
Ammunition:	42 x 120mm, 4750 x 7.62mm

MARDER

First production vehicles of the Marder were delivered to the German Army in December 1970 and production continued until 1975. The chassis remained in production for the Roland SAM system until 1983. The driver sits left front with one infantryman behind him, with the engine compartment to his right. The troop compartment is in the rear with three infantrymen seated each side. Many vehicles have a Milan anti-tank missile above the commander's hatch on the right side of the turret. The Marder has a number of distinctive features: a well-sloped glacis plate, hull sides that slope inwards above the suspension, a power-operated ramp in the hull rear, a large turret with sloping front, sides and rear with an externally mounted 20mm cannon and smoke grenade launchers to left of the cannon; and the suspension each side has six large evenly spaced road wheels. There are a number of variants: Marder 1A1 with double-feed for a 20mm cannon, image intensification night sight with thermal pointer, new water can racks and flaps for periscopes; Marder 1A1A, upgraded in all areas except passive night vision equipment; Marder 1A2 with modified chassis and suspension; and Marder 1A3. All Marders are being upgraded to the 1A3 standard with improved armour and new roof hatch arrangement.

SPECIFICATIONS

Type:	*infantry combat vehicle*
Crew:	*3 + 6*
Weight:	*29,200kg (64,240lb)*
Length:	*6.79m (22.27ft)*
Height:	*2.98m (9.77ft)*
Width:	*3.24m (10.62ft)*
Ground Clearance:	*0.44m (1.44ft)*
Vertical Obstacle:	*1m (3.28ft)*
Trench:	*2.5m (8.2ft)*
Gradient:	*60 percent*
Powerplant:	*MTU MB 833 Ea 500 diesel*
Power Rating:	*600hp*
Speed – Maximum:	*65km/h (40.62mph)*
Cruising Range:	*520km (325 miles)*
Main Armament:	*1 x 20mm*
Secondary Armament:	*1 x 7.62mm, 1 x Milan*
Ammunition:	*1250 x 20mm, 5000 x 7.62mm*

MARS

ARS is the German version of the Multiple Launch Rocket System (MLRS). Entering service with the German Army in 1990, it is a high-mobility automatic system based on an M270 weapons platform. MLRS fires surface-to-surface rockets and the Army Tactical Missile System (ATACMS). Without leaving the cab, the crew of three (driver, gunner and section chief) can fire up to 12 MLRS rockets in less than 60 seconds. The MLRS launcher unit comprises an M270 Launcher loaded with 12 rockets, packaged in two six-rocket pods. The launcher, which is mounted on a stretched Bradley chassis, is a highly automated self-loading and self-aiming system. It contains a fire control computer that integrates the vehicle and rocket launching operations. The rockets can be fired individually or in ripples of 2 to 12. Accuracy is maintained in all firing modes because the computer re-aims the launcher between rounds. The MLRS can be transported to the area of operations by C-5 transport aircraft or by train. The basic MLRS tactical rocket warhead contains 644 M77 munitions, which are dispensed above the target in mid-air. The dual-purpose bomblets are armed during freefall and a simple drag ribbon orients the bomblets for impact. Each MLRS launcher can deliver almost 8000 munitions in less than a minute.

SPECIFICATIONS

Type:	*multiple launch rocket system*
Crew:	*3*
Weight:	*24,756kg (54,463lb)*
Length:	*7.16m (23.49ft)*
Height:	*2.57m (8.43ft)*
Width:	*2.97m (9.74ft)*
Ground Clearance:	*0.43m (1.41ft)*
Vertical Obstacle:	*0.61m (2ft)*
Trench:	*1.68m (5.51ft)*
Gradient:	*60 percent*
Powerplant:	*Detroit Diesel 6V53TIA*
Power Rating:	*500hp*
Speed – Maximum:	*64km/h (40mph)*
Cruising Range:	*480km (300 miles)*
Main Armament:	*12 rockets*
Secondary Armament:	*none*
Ammunition:	*none*

PZH 2000

The PzH 2000 (*Panzerhaubitze* 2000) is the 155mm self-propelled howitzer developed for the German Army. The first system was delivered in July 1998 and the total German Army requirement is expected to be around 450 units. The gun has a chromium-plated barrel and semi-automatic lifting breech block with integrated 32-round standard primer magazine. Gun parameters such as chamber temperature are monitored automatically. The PzH 2000 is equipped with a fully automatic shell loading system with an ammunition management system which can handle 60 rounds of 155mm ammunition in total. The shells are picked up from the back of the vehicle and automatically stowed in the 60-round magazine in the centre of the chassis. This gives an impressive rate of fire of 3 rounds in less than 10 seconds and loading of 60 shells by two operators within 12 minutes, including the collation of ammunition data. The PzH 2000 can use an automatic mode of operation, including the data radio link with an external command and control system. Using the automatic mode, target engagements can be carried out by a crew of two. Using the fire control data provided by the ballistics computer, the gun is automatically laid and relayed during the fire mission. Overall the PzH 2000 is an excellent mobile artillery platform.

SPECIFICATIONS

Type:	self-propelled howitzer
Crew:	5
Weight:	55 000kg (121,000lb)
Length (Gun Forward):	11.67m (38.28ft)
Height:	3.06m (10ft)
Width:	3.58m (11.74ft)
Ground Clearance:	0.4m (1.31ft)
Vertical Obstacle:	1m (3.28ft)
Trench:	3m (9.84ft)
Gradient:	50 percent
Powerplant:	MTU MT 881 Ka 500 diesel
Power Rating:	1000hp
Speed – Maximum:	60km/h (37.5mph)
Cruising Range:	420km (262 miles)
Main Armament:	1 x 155mm
Secondary Armament:	1 x 7.62mm
Ammunition:	60 x 155mm, 1000 x 7.62mm

WIESEL

The Wiesel 1 weapons carrier is based on a Porsche concept. Rheinmetall was the general contractor for the production and delivery of both Wiesel 1 versions to the German Airborne Brigades. Firepower, mobility and excellent means of survival characterize the Wiesel 1, as well as air transportability, flexibility and quick operational readiness. In addition, it has good all-round observation and target reconnaissance facilities and night combat ability. The TOW version has a crew of three men and, due to its anti-tank missile system, can hit targets accurately at ranges up to 3750m (12,203ft). The Wiesel 2 multi-purpose carrier was developed from the Wiesel 1, specifically with the requirement for more room and loading capacity due to the army's extended range of missions, i.e. for rapid-reaction and peacekeeping missions. The air transportability, light weight, high mobility and low silhouette of its predecessor were kept in all vehicle versions, but the length was increased by the size of one pair of road wheels. This resulted in twice as much space in the interior of the vehicle. Both systems complement each other perfectly in their ability to fulfil a broad spectrum of missions. They can be air transported as internal or external loads on helicopters and as internal loads on fixed-wing aircraft.

SPECIFICATIONS

Type:	airportable armoured vehicle
Crew:	3
Weight:	2800kg (6160lb)
Length:	3.31m (10.85kg)
Height:	1.89m (6.2ft)
Width:	1.82m (5.97ft)
Ground Clearance:	0.3m (0.98ft)
Vertical Obstacle:	0.4m (1.31ft)
Trench:	1.2m (3.93ft)
Gradient:	60 percent
Powerplant:	VW turbocharged diesel
Power Rating:	86hp
Speed – Maximum:	75km/h (46.87mph)
Cruising Range:	300km (187 miles)
Main Armament:	1 x TOW ATGW launcher
Secondary Armament:	none
Ammunition:	7 x TOW ATGW

AS90

The AS90 is a 155mm self-propelled howitzer which entered service with the British Army in 1992. The crew consists of the driver plus four or three operators in the cupola: a commander, a gun layer and an ammunition loader. An automated loading system enables the gun to fire with a burst rate of 3 rounds in under 10 seconds, an intense rate of 6 rounds per minute in three minutes and a sustained rate of 2 rounds per minute. The gun, which does not require stabilizing spades, is equipped with a recoil and hydrogas suspension system which allows the turret to traverse and fire through the full 360 degrees. A dynamic reference unit (DRU) and electronic compensation for tilt of the vehicle are used for accurate orientation of the weapon system. The range is 24.7km (15.43 miles) using conventional ammunition. Fitting a 52-calibre barrel instead of the standard 39-calibre extends the range beyond 40km (25 miles). An automated ammunition handling system is included in the current upgrade programme. The vehicle is of all-welded steel armour construction which is rated to withstand impact by 7.62mm and 14.5mm armour-piercing shells and 152mm shell fragments. A system for increased ballistic protection against top attack by current generation anti-tank missiles is being developed.

SPECIFICATIONS

Type:	self-propelled howitzer
Crew:	4–5
Weight:	42,000kg (92,400lb)
Length (Gun Forward):	9.7m (31.82ft)
Height:	3m (9.84ft)
Width:	3.3m (10.82ft)
Ground Clearance:	0.4m (1.31ft)
Vertical Obstacle:	0.75m (2.46ft)
Trench:	2.8m (9.18ft)
Gradient:	60 percent
Powerplant:	Cummins V8 diesel
Power Rating:	660hp
Speed – Maximum:	55km/h (34.37mph)
Cruising Range:	350km (219 miles)
Main Armament:	1 x 155mm
Secondary Armament:	1 x 12.7mm
Ammunition:	48 x 155mm, 1000 x 12.7mm

CHALLENGER 1

The Challenger main battle tank is a development of the Centurion/Chieftain line, modified to produce the Shir/Iran 2 originally planned for service with the Iranian Army. After the Iranian Revolution and the fall of the Shah, the Shir/Iran 2 project was taken over by the British Army and the end result was Challenger, later redesignated as Challenger 1. The main differences between Challenger 1 and its predecessor Chieftain are the engine, which produces 1200bhp at 2300rpm, far more powerful than the Chieftain engine, and the Chobham armour, which gives very high protection levels against anti-armour weapons. The Challenger 1 had been completely replaced by the Challenger 2 by the end of 2001, and some Challenger 1 hulls will be used for specialist vehicles. The Challenger has a 12-cylinder 1200hp Perkins diesel engine and a David Brown TN54 gearbox, with six forward and two reverse gears. The maximum speed by road is 59km/h (36.87mph) and 40km/h (25mph) cross country. As well as the main and secondary armaments, the tank is equipped with two five-shot smoke grenade dischargers mounted in the turret. The tank also has a full nuclear, biological and chemical (NBC) defence system, and the commander, gunner and driver have access to night-vision equipment.

SPECIFICATIONS

Type:	main battle tank
Crew:	4
Weight:	62,000kg (136,400lb)
Length (Gun Forward):	11.55mm (37.89ft)
Height:	2.49m (8.16ft)
Width:	3.51m (11.51ft)
Ground Clearance:	0.5m (1.64ft)
Vertical Obstacle:	0.9m (2.95ft)
Trench:	2.8m (9.18ft)
Gradient:	58 percent
Powerplant:	Perkins Condor CV12 diesel
Power Rating:	1200hp
Speed – Maximum:	59km/h (36.87mph)
Cruising Range:	450km (281 miles)
Main Armament:	1 x 120mm
Secondary Armament:	2 x 7.62mm
Ammunition:	64 x 120mm, 4000 x 7.62mm

CHALLENGER 2

Challenger 2 is an advanced main battle tank which is in service with the British Army and with the Royal Army of Oman. Challenger 2 is equipped with an L30 120mm rifled tank gun, which is made from electro-slag refined steel (ESR) and is insulated with a thermal sleeve. It is fitted with a muzzle reference system and fume extraction. The turret is capable of 360-degree rotation and the weapon elevation range is from –10 to +20 degrees. There is capacity for 50 120mm projectiles, including armour-piercing, fin-stabilized, discarding sabot (APFSDS), high-explosive, squash head (HESH) or smoke rounds. The L30 gun can also fire the depleted uranium (DU) round with a stick charge propellant. With the DU round, the L30 is part of the Charm 1 gun, charge and projectile system. A Charm 3 system is under development in which the DU projectile has a higher length to diameter aspect ratio for increased penetration. Challenger 2E, the latest development model, has a new integrated weapon control and battlefield management system, which includes a gyrostabilized day/thermal sight for both commander and gunner. This allows hunter/killer operations with a common engagement sequence. An optional servo-controlled overhead weapons platform can also be fitted.

SPECIFICATIONS

Type:	main battle tank
Crew:	4
Weight:	62,500kg (137,500lb)
Length (Gun Forward):	11.55mm (37.89ft)
Height:	2.49m (8.16ft)
Width:	3.51m (11.51ft)
Ground Clearance:	0.5m (1.64ft)
Vertical Obstacle:	0.9m (2.95ft)
Trench:	2.8m (9.18ft)
Gradient:	60 percent
Powerplant:	Perkins Condor CV12 diesel
Power Rating:	1200hp
Speed – Maximum:	59km/h (36.87mph)
Cruising Range:	450km (281 miles)
Main Armament:	1 x 120mm
Secondary Armament:	2 x 7.62mm
Ammunition:	50 x 120mm, 4000 x 7.62mm

CHIEFTAIN

Around 900 Chieftains were built for the British Army with production being completed in the early 1970s. Although it is no longer in British frontline service, it is one of the great tanks of the twentieth century. There are a number of specialized variants of the tank which are still in service with the British Army. These include the Armoured Vehicle Royal Engineer (AVRE designated FV4203), Armoured Repair and Recovery Vehicle (ARRV), Armoured Recovery Vehicle (ARV designated FV4204) and Armoured Vehicle-Launched Bridge (AVLB designated FV4205), which carries the No. 8 or No. 9 Tank Bridge. Iran ordered 707 Chieftains in 1971 (Mk. 3/3(P) and Mk. 5/3(P)) with a number of armoured recovery vehicles and bridgelayers. Iran also took delivery of some 187 improved Chieftains, designated the FV4030/1. Oman bought a number of Chieftain Mk 15s (named *Qayd Al Ardh*) in the mid-1980s. The hull of the Chieftain is made of cast and rolled steel sections welded together. The Chieftain mounts a Royal Ordnance 120mm L11A5 rifled gun fitted with a Pilkington Optronics laser rangefinder. In the 1970s, British Army Chieftains were fitted with the thermal observation and gunnery sight (TOGS), a fully integrated improved fire control system and Stillbrew armour.

SPECIFICATIONS

Type:	*main battle tank*
Crew:	*4*
Weight:	*53,500kg (117,700lb)*
Length (Gun Forward):	*10.79m (35.4ft)*
Height:	*2.89m (9.48ft)*
Width:	*3.5m (11.48ft)*
Ground Clearance:	*0.5m (1.64ft)*
Vertical Obstacle:	*0.91m (2.98ft)*
Trench:	*3.14m (10.3ft)*
Gradient:	*60 percent*
Powerplant:	*Leyland L60 diesel*
Power Rating:	*750hp*
Speed – Maximum:	*48km/h (30mph)*
Cruising Range:	*500km (312 miles)*
Main Armament:	*1 x 120mm*
Secondary Armament:	*2 x 7.62mm, 1 x 12.7mm*
Ammunition:	*64 x 120mm, 6000 x 7.62mm*

FV 430

First introduced in 1962, the FV 430 series of armoured vehicles was developed to fulfil no less than 14 roles including command post armoured personnel carrier, ambulance, minelayer, recovery and repair vehicle, mortar carrier, radar or troop carrier. Totally NBC proof, it can carry up to 10 men and 2 crew and may be armed with a 7.62mm machine gun or turret-mounted L37 machine gun. The FV 432 will continue to provide the bulk of armoured transport for the British Army until replaced in the twenty-first century, probably with another vehicle with the same capacity (complete replacement with the Warrior infantry fighting vehicle would require an expanded fleet of vehicles as the Warrior's capacity is not as good). There are a number of variants of this vehicle: the FV 434 is a engineer vehicle with a crane capable of lifting an AFV engine pack. It includes a field repair kit and has a total carrying ability of 2703kg (5947lb). The crane has a radius of 2.25m (7.38ft) and can lift 3050kg (6710lb). The FV 439 is used by the Royal Signals as a mobile command post; it is a command type FV 432 fitted with extra radios and an erectable mast. The signals equipment is carried internally, with external mast ready for erection and extra stowage bins mounted externally on the vehicle.

SPECIFICATIONS

Type:	armoured personnel carrier
Crew:	2 + 10
Weight:	15,280kg (33,616lb)
Length:	5.25m (17.22ft)
Height:	2.28m (7.48ft)
Width:	2.8m (9.18ft)
Ground Clearance:	0.5m (1.64ft)
Vertical Obstacle:	0.9m (2.95ft)
Trench:	2.05m (6.72ft)
Gradient:	60 percent
Powerplant:	Rolls-Royce K60 diesel
Power Rating:	240hp
Speed – Maximum:	52km/h (32.5mph)
Cruising Range:	580km (362 miles)
Main Armament:	1 x 7.62mm
Secondary Armament:	3 x smoke dischargers
Ammunition:	unknown

SABRE

Sabre was brought into service in 1995 using a Scorpion chassis and the 30mm turret from the Combat Vehicle Reconnaissance (Tracked) (CVR(T)) Fox. It is almost identical to Scimitar but has a lower profile turret. Sabre is used by the British Army for close reconnaissance and is equipped with a Rarden Cannon and Hughes 7.62mm chain gun. In 1997 the Cummins Engine Company was chosen by the UK Ministry of Defence to supply diesel engines to re-power the British Army's fleet of Combat Vehicle Reconnaissance (Tracked) light armoured vehicles. The announcement, made on the opening day of the Royal Navy/British Army Equipment Exhibition (31 September), revealed that vehicles would be fitted with the Cummins B-series six-cylinder, 5.9-litre engine for Reliability Demonstration Trials. This was the first stage in a pro-gramme which will eventually see over 1300 CVR(T)s – which include Scimitar, Sabre, Samson, Sultan and Samaritan vehicles – re-engined. Cummins will develop the vehicle conversion kit for all variants. The army's family of CVR(T) vehicles, designed and produced by Alvis Vehicles, were the last British Army armoured fighting vehicles to be powered by a petrol engine. Around 140 Sabres are currently in service with the British Army.

SPECIFICATIONS

Type:	reconnaissance vehicle
Crew:	3
Weight:	8130kg (17,886lb)
Length (Gun Forward):	5.15m (16.89ft)
Height:	2.17m (7.11ft)
Width:	2.17m (7.11ft)
Ground Clearance:	0.35m (1.14ft)
Vertical Obstacle:	0.5m (1.64ft)
Trench:	2.05m (6.72ft)
Gradient:	60 percent
Powerplant:	Cummins BTA diesel
Power Rating:	190hp
Speed – Maximum:	80.5km/h (50.3mph)
Cruising Range:	644km (403 miles)
Main Armament:	1 x 30mm
Secondary Armament:	1 x 7.62mm
Ammunition:	40 x 30mm, 3000 x 7.62mm

SCIMITAR

The Scimitar is a variant of the Scorpion armoured reconnaissance vehicle which continues to serve in the British Army even though it is tactically obsolete. Some Scorpions have since been converted to the Scimitar configuration using 30mm Rarden turrets of the obsolete Fox armoured car. The Scimitar's 30mm Rarden gun is powerful enough to defeat enemy armoured reconnaissance vehicles and personnel carriers. Used by medium reconnaissance regiments and armoured infantry units for reconnaissance, the vehicle's weapon is mainly for self-defence. In the attack, a patrol of two Scimitars may provide fire support against a bridge or similar objective. In 2000, the Scimitar fleet underwent a Life Extension Programme (LEP). The major part of this upgrade was the replacement of the current Jaguar 4.2-litre petrol engine by a more fuel-efficient Cummins BTA 5.9-litre diesel engine developing 190hp, although there were some additional modifications. The LEP was carried out on the Scimitar and Sabre reconnaissance vehicles, Spartan armoured personnel carrier, Sultan command post vehicle, Samson recovery vehicle, Samaritan ambulance and the Striker anti-tank vehicle armed with Swingfire anti-tank missiles. Fast and with good viewing equipment, it is an ideal reconnaissance vehicle.

SPECIFICATIONS

Type:	reconnaissance vehicle
Crew:	3
Weight:	8070kg (17,754lb)
Length (Gun Forward):	5.15m (16.89ft)
Height:	2.1m (6.88ft)
Width:	2.2m (7.21ft)
Ground Clearance:	0.35m (1.14ft)
Vertical Obstacle:	0.5m (1.64ft)
Trench:	2.05m (6.72ft)
Gradient:	60 percent
Powerplant:	Cummins BTA diesel
Power Rating:	190hp
Speed – Maximum:	80km/h (50mph)
Cruising Range:	644km (403 miles)
Main Armament:	1 x 30mm
Secondary Armament:	1 x 7.62mm
Ammunition:	160 x 30mm, 3000 x 7.62mm

SCORPION

The veteran Scorpion reconnaissance vehicle was the first of the British Army's Combat Vehicle Reconnaissance (Tracked) (CVR(T)) family, and was originally developed to meet a British Army requirement for a tracked reconnaissance vehicle. The first production units were completed in 1972 armed with a 76mm gun and powered by a Jaguar 4.2-litre petrol engine. Since then Alvis has built more than 3000 Scorpion vehicles for the home and export market. The latest production model is powered by a more fuel-efficient diesel engine (Cummins) and is fitted with a Cockerill 90mm gun. A wide range of optional equipment is available including an NBC (nuclear, biological, chemical) protection system, image intensification or thermal night vision equipment, a powered turret, navigation system, air-conditioning system and flotation screens. The Scorpion light tank is in service with Belgium, Botswana, Brunei, Chile, Honduras, Indonesia, Iran, Ireland, Jordan, Malaysia, Nigeria, Oman, the Philippines, Spain, Tanzania, Thailand, Togo, United Arab Emirates and Great Britain. This includes both 76mm and 90mm versions and variants. The Scorpion was originally designed as a fully amphibious vehicle with preparation, but this ability was subsequently removed from British Army Scorpions.

SPECIFICATIONS

Type:	reconnaissance vehicle
Crew:	3
Weight:	8073kg (17,761lb)
Length (Gun Forward):	4.79m (15.71ft)
Height:	2.1m (6.88ft)
Width:	2.23m (7.54ft)
Ground Clearance:	0.35m (1.14ft)
Vertical Obstacle:	0.5m (1.64ft)
Trench:	2.05m (6.72ft)
Gradient:	60 percent
Powerplant:	Cummins BTA diesel
Power Rating:	190hp
Speed – Maximum:	80.5km/h (50.3mph)
Cruising Range:	644km (403 miles)
Main Armament:	1 x 76mm
Secondary Armament:	1 x 7.62mm
Ammunition:	40 x 76mm, 3000 x 7.62mm

SPARTAN

partan is a derivative of the CVR(T) vehicle (Combat Vehicle Reconnaissance (Tracked). The vehicles all shared the same engine, chassis and were made almost entirely of aluminum. The Spartan was the armoured personnel carrier (APC) of the series and was named thus due to the absence of turret and armament (other than the machine gun mounted for defensive purposes). The vehicle is small, and can only carry a maximum of four troops in its personnel compartment. Spartan is used by specialist troops which can include mortar fire control teams, or anti-aircraft teams equipped with Javelin missiles, or it can serve as an engineer command vehicle. Spartan is in use with a number of countries, and the design will serve well into this century. In 2000, for example, the Belgian Ministry of Defence delivered the first 50 of 100 ex-Belgian Army Spartan armoured personnel carrier variants to the Jordanian armed forces. The King Hussein Main Workshops in Zarqa have overhauled the first batch, which will shortly be issued to field units, including, it is believed, the élite Special Operations Command. The green and black camouflage pattern normally associated with operations in northwest Europe has been retained, as has the Spartan's original 190hp Jaguar 4.2-litre petrol engine.

SPECIFICATIONS

Type:	armoured personnel carrier
Crew:	3 + 4
Weight:	8172kg (17,978lb)
Length:	5.12m (16.79ft)
Height:	2.26m (7.41ft)
Width:	2.24m (7.34ft)
Ground Clearance:	0.35m (1.14ft)
Vertical Obstacle:	0.5m (1.64ft)
Trench:	2.05m (6.72ft)
Gradient:	60 percent
Powerplant:	Jaguar J60 No. 1 petrol
Power Rating:	190hp
Speed – Maximum:	80.5km/h (50.3mph)
Cruising Range:	483km (302 miles)
Main Armament:	1 x 7.62mm
Secondary Armament:	none
Ammunition:	3000 x 7.62mm

STARSTREAK

The Starstreak self-propelled high-velocity missile (SP HVM) system has been in service with the British Army since 1997. The missile consists of a two-stage solid propellant rocket motor, a separation system and three high-density darts. A pulse of power from the missile firing unit causes the first-stage motor to ignite, which accelerates the missile. Canted nozzles on the missile cause it to roll. The centrifugal force of the roll causes the fins to unfold for aerodynamic stability in flight. Once clear of the canister, the motor is jettisoned. The second-stage motor ignites and accelerates the missile to a velocity greater than Mach 4. A separation system at the front end of the motor contains three darts. The Starstreak SP HVM is mounted on a tracked Stormer vehicle. The system has eight rounds of Starstreak missiles ready to fire, with a further 12 missiles carried. The SP HVM is fitted with a roof-mounted Air Defence Alerting Device (ADAD), whose infrared scanner and processor provide target detection and prioritization and the system automatically slews the weapon sight onto the target. The use of ADAD requires that the vehicle be, briefly, stationary. A panoramic weapon sight is located at the front right of the vehicle. Thales Optronics has been awarded a contract to supply a new thermal sighting system for the British Army.

SPECIFICATIONS

Type:	self-propelled SAM
Crew:	3
Weight:	12,700kg (27,940lb)
Length:	5.27m (17.29ft)
Height:	3m (9.84ft)
Width:	2.76m (9ft)
Ground Clearance:	0.42m (1.37ft)
Vertical Obstacle:	0.6m (1.96ft)
Trench:	1.75m (5.74ft)
Gradient:	60 percent
Powerplant:	Perkins T6 diesel
Power Rating:	250hp
Speed – Maximum:	80km/h (50mph)
Cruising Range:	650km (406 miles)
Main Armament:	8 x Starstreak
Secondary Armament:	none
Ammunition:	12 x Starstreak

STORMER

Alvis Vehicles built the original Stormer armoured personnel carrier (APC), then known as the FV 433, in the 1970s using components of its Scorpion Combat Vehicle Reconnaissance (Tracked) range. Production of the Stormer began in 1982: three for the USA to evaluate and 25 for Malaysia to use in an armoured personnel carrier role. The British Army, which selected Stormer in 1986 to carry the Starstreak system, uses three versions of the vehicle: as a platform for the Starstreak system, a reconnaissance vehicle for Starstreak units, and a flatbed fitted with the Alliant Techsystems Volcano anti-tank mine-scattering system. Stormer can use various weapon systems, such as a two-person turret armed with a 25mm cannon. There is a wide range of optional equipment, including an NBC protection system, an amphibious kit, passive night-vision equipment, and an air-conditioning system. Indonesia is the newest Stormer customer and has received a number of variants, including the armoured personnel carrier, command post vehicle, ambulance, recovery, bridgelayer and logistics vehicle. Stormer is in use with a number of countries: Indonesia (50); Malaysia (25); Oman (4); and Great Britain (170 plus still on delivery). The only APC users are Indonesia and Malaysia.

SPECIFICATIONS

Type:	*armoured personnel carrier*
Crew:	*1 + 12*
Weight:	*12,700kg (27,940lb)*
Length:	*5.27m (17.29ft)*
Height:	*2.49m (8.16ft)*
Width:	*2.7m (9ft)*
Ground Clearance:	*0.42m (1.37ft)*
Vertical Obstacle:	*0.6m (1.96ft)*
Trench:	*1.75m (5.74ft)*
Gradient:	*60 percent*
Powerplant:	*Perkins T6/3544 diesel*
Power Rating:	*250hp*
Speed – Maximum:	*80km/h (50mph)*
Cruising Range:	*650km (406 miles)*
Main Armament:	*1 x 7.62mm*
Secondary Armament:	*none*
Ammunition:	*3000 x 7.62mm*

STORMER 30

Stormer 30 is a new variant of the Stormer family of tracked vehicles. The development was based on proven technology from the Scorpion range of light tanks for operation on any terrain and in any environment. The vehicle is operated by three crew members: the driver, a commander/loader and the gunner. The main armament of the Stormer 30 is the Boeing Bushmaster II 30mm automatic cannon. The rate of fire of the cannon is from single shot to a maximum of 200 rounds per minute. The cannon has a double selection ammunition feed system with 180 rounds of ammunition ready to fire. Stormer 30 is also equipped with a 7.62mm general purpose machine gun with a range of 400m (1312ft), which is mounted coaxially with the main armament and has 700 rounds of ready-to-fire ammunition. Two multi-barrel grenade launchers installed on the front of the turret provide 180-degree coverage over the forward arc. The launchers, operating on the 24V electrical supply, are each armed with four smoke grenades. The sighting and vision systems are fitted according to the customer country's mission requirements. The commander's station is fitted with an optional panoramic sight and six episcopes fitted with a switch for gun and episcope alignment. The gunner's station is equipped with a day and night sight.

SPECIFICATIONS

Type:	light tank
Crew:	3
Weight:	13,000kg (28,600lb)
Length:	5.27m (17.29ft)
Height:	2.49m (8.16ft)
Width:	2.7m (9ft)
Ground Clearance:	0.42m (1.37ft)
Vertical Obstacle:	0.6m (1.96ft)
Trench:	1.75m (5.74ft)
Gradient:	60 percent
Powerplant:	Cummins 6B-275
Power Rating:	275hp
Speed – Maximum:	80km/h (50mph)
Cruising Range:	400km (250 miles)
Main Armament:	1 x 30mm
Secondary Armament:	2 x TOW, 1 x 7.62mm
Ammunition:	180 x 30mm, 700 x 7.62mm

STRIKER

Striker is a CVR(T) vehicle with a primary role to destroy enemy armour. Striker carries a total of 10 Swingfire anti-tank missiles with a range of up to 4km (2.5 miles). Five of these missiles are carried in bins on top of the vehicle; however, these need to be reloaded from outside the vehicle. This requires one of the crew operating outside the vehicle, making him very vulnerable to enemy small-arms fire. The ubiquitous FV 432 has been converted to carry the Swingfire missile system as an anti-tank weapon system, with the cupola mounted at the rear and the missile bins behind it to the left. The vehicle is manufactured with an armoured aluminium hull with spaced high-hardness steel armour and a spall liner which provide protection against 14.5mm heavy machine-gun rounds and artillery shell splinters. The Striker vehicle is equipped with a full nuclear, biological and chemical (NBC) weapons defence capability, and the allocation of night-vision devices allows its crew to operate on the 24-hour battlefield. For self-defence the Striker is equipped with two four-shot smoke grenade dischargers, plus a 7.62mm machine gun for close-in defence against infantry. The vehicle carries 3000 rounds of ammunition for the machine gun. The petrol engine is fed from a 350-litre fuel tank.

SPECIFICATIONS

Type:	anti-tank vehicle
Crew:	3
Weight:	8172kg (17,978lb)
Length:	5.12m (16.79ft)
Height:	2.26m (7.41ft)
Width:	2.24m (7.34ft)
Ground Clearance:	0.35m (1.14ft)
Vertical Obstacle:	0.5m (1.64ft)
Trench:	2.05m (6.72ft)
Gradient:	60 percent
Powerplant:	Jaguar J60 No. 1 petrol
Power Rating:	190hp
Speed – Maximum:	80.5km/h (50.3mph)
Cruising Range:	483km (302 miles)
Main Armament:	5 x Swingfire
Secondary Armament:	1 x 7.62mm
Ammunition:	10 x Swingfire, 3000 x 7.62mm

TRACKED RAPIER

Rapier has become one of the most successful low-altitude mobile surface-to-air missiles (SAMs) ever deployed. Highly mobile and capable of being mounted on a trailer or on a tracked vehicle, Rapier showed its worth in the 1982 Falklands War when it knocked out Argentine aircraft. The missile itself is intended to destroy low-altitude, fast-moving threats as well as helicopters. Tracked Rapier is an armoured mobile air defence system carrying eight missiles on a trainable launcher with the guidance systems installed in an armoured cab. The system was originally developed for the Shah of Iran's Army, but like the Shir main battle tank, eventually found a home with the British Army. Blindfire Rapier is a radar-equipped version of the Rapier SAM defence system used by the RAF Regiment and British Army for point air defence. The operator still retains the option of optical targeting if the radar fails to lock onto the target, but if the radar is selected the engagement sequence is automatic. The radar has a range of about 12km (7.5 miles). The system is in constant development and can be made ready to fire in less than 15 seconds. The Rapier system proved an effective anti-aircraft missile during the 1982 Falklands War, and will continue in service well into the twenty-first century.

SPECIFICATIONS

Type:	self-propelled SAM
Crew:	3
Weight:	14,010kg (30,822lb)
Length:	6.4m (21ft)
Height:	2.78m (9.12ft)
Width:	2.8m (9.18ft)
Ground Clearance:	0.41m (1.34ft)
Vertical Obstacle:	0.6m (1.96ft)
Trench:	1.68m (5.51ft)
Gradient:	60 percent
Powerplant:	Detroit Diesel Model 6V-53
Power Rating:	210hp
Speed – Maximum:	48km/h (30mph)
Cruising Range:	300km (187 miles)
Main Armament:	8 x Rapier SAM
Secondary Armament:	none
Ammunition:	none

WARRIOR

The Warrior infantry fighting vehicle carries a driver, commander, gunner and seven fully equipped soldiers, together with supplies and weapons for a 48-hour period in NBC conditions. The Warrior adapts to a range of roles with weapon fits ranging from machine guns to 90mm guns, mortars and missile systems. The aluminium armour construction provides protection against 14.5mm armour-piercing rounds, 155mm air burst shell fragments and 9kg (19.8lb) anti-tank mines. Enhanced protection against other threats can be provided with applique armour. The reconnaissance version is fitted with additional armoured protection against conventional and chemical attack: armour shielding covers the front, sides and the suspension of the vehicle. The reconnaissance vehicle is normally operated by a crew of three – the driver, commander and the gunner – and also has the capacity to accommodate a reconnaissance officer and additional surveillance kit. The vehicle is equipped with an electrically operated turret which can traverse through a full 360 degrees. The turret is fitted with a Boeing M242 chain gun on a stabilized mount which allows the gun to be used while the vehicle is in motion. The turret also has an M240 7.62mm machine gun and TOW missile launchers are mounted on each side.

SPECIFICATIONS

Type:	infantry fighting vehicle
Crew:	3 + 7
Weight:	24,500kg (53,900lb)
Length (Gun Forward):	6.34m (20.8ft)
Height:	2.79m (9.15ft)
Width:	3.03m (9.94ft)
Ground Clearance:	0.49m (1.6ft)
Vertical Obstacle:	0.75m (2.46ft)
Trench:	2.5m (8.2ft)
Gradient:	60 percent
Powerplant:	Perkins CV8 TCA V-8 diesel
Power Rating:	550hp
Speed – Maximum:	75km/h (46.87mph)
Cruising Range:	660km (412 miles)
Main Armament:	1 x 30mm
Secondary Armament:	2 x TOW, 1 x 7.62mm
Ammunition:	250 x 30mm, 2000 x 7.62mm

MERKAVA 2

The Merkava is the innovative design of Major-General Israel Tal, whose primary criterion was crew survivability. For example, the engine is in the front to provide protection for the crew and there is a special protective umbrella for the tank commander to enable protection from indirect fire with the hatches open. Special "spaced armour" is in use along with protected fuel and ammunition compartments. Rear ammunition stowage is combined with a rear entrance and exit. Since the rounds are stowed in containers that can be removed from the vehicle whenever necessary, this space can accommodate tank crewmen who have been forced to abandon their vehicles, or even infantrymen. Rear ammunition stowage allows replenishment much more easily than if rounds have to be replaced in a carousel in the hull centre. Tank crews have long admired Merkava's rear entrance and exit, recognizing that it allows them to mount and dismount unobserved by the enemy and provides an excellent escape route. The gunner's station is equipped with a thermal sight and a day sight with a television channel, which are stabilized in two axes. A laser rangefinder and target tracker are integrated into the gunner's sight. The commander's station is fitted with a sight which can be optically relayed to the gunner's sight.

SPECIFICATIONS

Type:	*main battle tank*
Crew:	*4*
Weight:	*61,000kg (134,200lb)*
Length (Gun Forward):	*8.8m (28.87ft)*
Height:	*2.8m (9.18ft)*
Width:	*3.7m (12.13ft)*
Ground Clearance:	*0.47m (1.54ft)*
Vertical Obstacle:	*0.95m (3.11ft)*
Trench:	*3m (9.84ft)*
Gradient:	*70 percent*
Powerplant:	*1790-6A V-12 diesel*
Power Rating:	*900hp*
Speed – Maximum:	*46km/h (28.75mph)*
Cruising Range:	*400km (250 miles)*
Main Armament:	*1 x 105mm*
Secondary Armament:	*3 x 7.62mm, 1 x 60mm mortar*
Ammunition:	*62 x 105mm, 10,000 x 7.62mm*

MERKAVA 3

The Merkava Mk 3 entered service with the Israeli Army at the beginning of 1990. The main features of the Mk 3 are a new suspension system, a 1200hp engine and new transmission, a higher-power main gun, and new armour protection. Ballistic protection is provided by special armour modules, which are attached to the tank by bolts. About 1000 Merkava Mk 2 and Mk 3 tanks are in service with the Israeli armed forces. The main gun is a 120mm smoothbore gun developed by Israeli Military Industries. The gun has a Vidco Industries thermal sleeve, which increases accuracy by preventing distortion through the effects of weather, heat and shock. The tank is fitted with the Amcoram LWS-2 laser warning system, with the threat warning display installed at the commander's station. The turret and hull are fitted with a modular armour system which can be changed in the field. The forward section of the turret is fitted with additional blocks of armour to provide extra protection against the latest generation of top attack anti-tank missiles. A skirt of chains with ball weights is installed on the lower half of the turret bustle. Incoming high-explosive, anti-tank (HEAT) projectiles detonate on impact with the chains instead of penetrating the turret ring. Sprung armour side skirts protect the wheels and tracks.

SPECIFICATIONS

Type:	main battle tank
Crew:	4
Weight:	61,000kg (134,200lb)
Length (Gun Forward):	8.8m (28.87ft)
Height:	2.8m (9.18ft)
Width:	3.7m (12.13ft)
Ground Clearance:	0.47m (1.54ft)
Vertical Obstacle:	0.95m (3.11ft)
Trench:	3m (9.84ft)
Gradient:	70 percent
Powerplant:	AVDS-1790-9AR diesel
Power Rating:	1200hp
Speed – Maximum:	55km/h (34.37mph)
Cruising Range:	500km (312 miles)
Main Armament:	1 x 120mm
Secondary Armament:	3 x 7.62mm, 1 x 60mm mortar
Ammunition:	50 x 120mm, 10,000 x 7.62mm

ARIETE

The Italian Ariete tank can engage stationary and moving targets in both day and night conditions, while the tank itself is stationary or on the move. The main gun is a 120mm smoothbore gun which is fitted with a thermal sleeve, a fume extraction system and a muzzle reference system. The gun is stabilized in two axes by hydraulic servoes and can fire all available types of ammunition including armour-piercing, fin-stabilized, discarding sabot (APFSDS) and high explosive, anti-tank (HEAT) rounds. The hull and turret are of all-welded steel construction with enhanced armour protection over the frontal arc. The crew is protected from nuclear, biological and chemical (NBC) warfare by an NBC protection system. The tank's fire control system includes a day/night stabilized commander's panoramic periscope sight, gunner's stabilized sight with thermal imager and laser rangefinder, and digital fire control computer. The digital fire control computer downloads data from the tank's meteorological and wind sensors, together with the tank attitude, barrel wear characteristics, ammunition and target data. The computer calculates the fire control algorithms and is used to control the gun, the sighting systems and the laser rangefinder. Ariete is currently in service with the Italian Army.

SPECIFICATIONS

Type:	*main battle tank*
Crew:	*4*
Weight:	*54,000kg (118,800lb)*
Length (Gun Forward):	*9.67m (31.72ft)*
Height:	*2.5m (8.2ft)*
Width:	*3.6m (11.81ft)*
Ground Clearance:	*0.48m (1.57ft)*
Vertical Obstacle:	*2.1m (6.88ft)*
Trench:	*3m (9.84ft)*
Gradient:	*60 percent*
Powerplant:	*Iveco V-12 MTCA diesel*
Power Rating:	*1300hp*
Speed – Maximum:	*65km/h (40.62mph)*
Cruising Range:	*550km (344 miles)*
Main Armament:	*1 x 120mm*
Secondary Armament:	*2 x 7.62mm*
Ammunition:	*40 x 120mm, 2500 x 7.62mm*

DARDO

The Dardo infantry fighting vehicle has a 25mm gun turret, but can also be fitted with a 30 or 60mm gun turret. It is intended to be the basic model of a family of vehicles to include a 120mm mortar carrier, command vehicle, ambulance and light tank with a 105mm gun turret. The Dardo's main weapon is the 25mm cannon which has a rate of fire of 600 rounds per minute (200 rounds of ammunition are carried in the turret ready to fire). Two 7.62mm machine guns are installed on the turret, one coaxial with the main gun. Two TOW anti-tank guided weapon launchers are installed, one on each side of the turret. The TOW missile, supplied by Raytheon Missile Systems Company, is a wire-guided, optically tracked missile with a maximum range of 3.75km (2.34 miles). The hull is of all-welded aluminium alloy with add-on steel armour plates for increased protection. The vehicle has a very low profile, with height of 2.64m (8.66ft) to the top of the turret, which decreases the radar and visual signature of the vehicle for enhanced survivability. Smoke grenade launchers, with four 80mm barrels per side, are installed on the front of the turret on either side of the main gun in the forward pointing direction. The crew compartment has five rifle ports, two on each side plus one in the rear ramp, for close defence.

SPECIFICATIONS

Type:	infantry fighting vehicle
Crew:	3 + 6
Weight:	23,000kg (50,600lb)
Length:	6.7m (21.98ft)
Height:	2.64m (8.66ft)
Width:	3m (9.84ft)
Ground Clearance:	0.4m (1.31ft)
Vertical Obstacle:	0.85m (2.78ft)
Trench:	2.5m (8.2ft)
Gradient:	60 percent
Powerplant:	Iveco 8260 V-6 diesel
Power Rating:	520hp
Speed – Maximum:	70km/h (43.75mph)
Cruising Range:	500km (312 miles)
Main Armament:	1 x 25mm
Secondary Armament:	2 x 7.62mm, 2 x TOW
Ammunition:	200 x 25mm

TYPE 74

The Type 74 is armed with the British-designed 105mm L7 type rifled tank gun manufactured under licence. New 105mm APFSDS and high-explosive, anti-tank, missile projectile (HEATMP) rounds were developed for the Type 74. The hydropneumatic suspension system, including the attitude controls, make the vehicle excellent for operation over rugged Japanese terrain. The vertical variability of the road wheel positions provides superior suspension capabilities, and leading-edge technology was integrated into the gun control and targeting devices, comprised of computerized laser rangefinders, fire control systems and gun stabilization systems. The choice of an electrically powered gun turret was validated when the 1973 Middle East war demonstrated that hydraulic-driven tank turrets were susceptible to fire. The Type 74 tank is equipped with floodlights with xenon lamps instead of tungsten lamps (the initial design of the floodlight filter measured 60cm [23.62in] in diameter and broke easily from the shock or air blast each time the gun was fired). Night-vision operating systems are based on models obtained through technical aid from the United States, and consist of the periscope-type hanging from the hatch above the driver's head. The Type 74 is equipped with the ruby laser type laser rangefinder.

SPECIFICATIONS

Type:	main battle tank
Crew:	4
Weight:	38,000kg (83,600lb)
Length (Gun Forward):	9.42m (30.9ft)
Height:	2.48m (8.13ft)
Width:	3.18m (10.43ft)
Ground Clearance:	0.65m (2.13ft)
Vertical Obstacle:	1m (3.28ft)
Trench:	2.7m (8.85ft)
Gradient:	60 percent
Powerplant:	Mitsubishi 10ZF Type 22 diesel
Power Rating:	720hp
Speed – Maximum:	55km/h (46.87mph)
Cruising Range:	300km (187 miles)
Main Armament:	1 x 105mm
Secondary Armament:	1 x 7.62mm, 1 x 12.7mm
Ammunition:	55 x 105mm, 4500 x 7.62mm

TYPE 90

Development of the Type 90 tank started in 1977, and it was accepted for service in 1990. The tank is equipped with the same Rheinmetall 120mm tank gun as the German Leopard 2. It carries a smoothbore barrel rather than a rifled barrel, and ammunition includes armour-piercing projectiles, anti-tank howitzer shells, and adhesive – high explosive plastic (HEP) – howitzer shells. With the exception of the turretless Swedish Stridsvagn (S-type) tank and various Russian models, the Type 90 tank is the first tank to achieve manpower savings by reducing the crew to three through the development of an ammunition autoloader. Innovative technology includes a laser and thermal-guided gun and turret controls. The automatic target tracking system using a thermal image display is controlled through the tank commander's targeting periscope attached to the top of the turret in an independently rotatable mode. Night-vision rangefinders are integrated into fire control systems and night-vision thermal imaging systems of a passive type use the infrared rays emitted from the opposing target to increase accuracy. These features enable the tank to achieve high-precision, mobile firing. Proprietary technology was used on the composite armour, including steel and ceramics with superior projectile-resistant qualities.

SPECIFICATIONS

Type:	*main battle tank*
Crew:	*3*
Weight:	*50,000kg (110,000lb)*
Length (Gun Forward):	*9.75m (31.98ft)*
Height:	*2.34m (7.67ft)*
Width:	*3.42m (11.22ft)*
Ground Clearance:	*0.45m (1.47ft)*
Vertical Obstacle:	*1m (3.28ft)*
Trench:	*2.7m (8.85ft)*
Gradient:	*60 percent*
Powerplant:	*Mitsubishi 10ZG diesel*
Power Rating:	*1500hp*
Speed – Maximum:	*70km/h (43.75mph)*
Cruising Range:	*400km (250 miles)*
Main Armament:	*1 x 120mm*
Secondary Armament:	*1 x 7.62mm, 1 x 12.7mm*
Ammunition:	*unknown*

2S1 M1974

Ever since the 2S1 was seen in public for the first time in 1974, it has been known under the provisional designation M1974. It also has been referred to as SP-74 and SAU-122. Although the 2S1 has been variously described as a gun, a gun-howitzer or a howitzer, the Soviet press called it a howitzer. The boat-like hull contains the engine compartment at the right front and the driver's compartment at the left front, with the driver's hatch to the left of the gun tube. The fighting compartment in the rear of the hull is topped by a low-silhouette, rotating turret. Atop the all-welded turret are the commander's cupola (with single hatch cover) on the left and the loader's hatch on the right. The gunner, also located in the left side of the turret, has no hatch. The commander and driver have infrared night-sighting equipment, but there is no infrared gunnery equipment. An interesting feature on the turret is the teardrop-shaped port cover on the left front near the gunner's position. The 2S1 has a direct fire sight besides its panoramic telescope and it is fitted with a collective NBC overpressure and filtration protective system. The 122mm howitzer mounted on the rounded front of the turret is derived from the towed howitzer D-30. The double-baffle muzzle brake is flush with the forward edge of the hull.

SPECIFICATIONS

Type:	self-propelled gun
Crew:	4
Weight:	15,700kg (34,540lb)
Length (Gun Forward):	7.26m (23.81ft)
Height:	2.72m (8.92ft)
Width:	2.85m (9.35ft)
Ground Clearance:	0.4m (1.31ft)
Vertical Obstacle:	0.7m (2.29ft)
Trench:	2.75m (9.02ft)
Gradient:	77 percent
Powerplant:	YaMZ-238 diesel
Power Rating:	300hp
Speed – Maximum:	60km/h (37.5mph)
Cruising Range:	500km (312 miles)
Main Armament:	1 x 122mm
Secondary Armament:	none
Ammunition:	40 x 122mm

2S3 M1973

SPECIFICATIONS

The 2S3 was first introduced into the Soviet inventory in 1973 and has also been known under the provisional designation M1973. The 2S3 comprises a modified version of the 152mm towed howitzer D-20 and a chassis similar to the SA-4/Ganef launch vehicle. The thick gun tube extends beyond the front of the hull (the length of the double-baffle muzzle brake). It differs from the D-20 by the addition of a bore evacuator just behind the muzzle brake and, in travel position, it is supported by a brace attached just behind the bore evacuator. The 2S3 provides highly mobile, all-terrain fire support for motorized rifle and tank divisions, though is now a little old and outmoded. Its maximum range with a normal round is the same as that of the 152mm towed howitzer D-20 – 17.2km (10.75 miles) – and it also fires a long-range round, increasing its range to about 30km (18.75 miles). The 2S3M is an upgrade version of the 2S3. The 2S3M turret contains the 2A33 cannon, fire control equipment, ammunition storage space and work positions for commander, gunner and loader. The cannon extends beyond the vehicle front and has an electrical loader/rammer attached to the cradle. Ammunition is stored in the rear of the chassis and can be replenished through a hatch in the rear panel.

Type:	self-propelled gun
Crew:	4
Weight:	27,500kg (60,500lb)
Length (Gun Forward):	7.75m (25.42ft)
Height:	3.13m (10.26ft)
Width:	3.21m (10.53ft)
Ground Clearance:	0.45m (1.47ft)
Vertical Obstacle:	0.7m (2.29ft)
Trench:	3m (9.84ft)
Gradient:	60 percent
Powerplant:	V-59 V-12 water-cooled diesel
Power Rating:	520hp
Speed – Maximum:	60km/h (37.5mph)
Cruising Range:	450km (281 miles)
Main Armament:	1 x 152mm
Secondary Armament:	1 x 7.62mm
Ammunition:	46 x 152mm, 1500 x 7.62mm

2S19 MSTA-S

The 152mm 2S19 MSTA-S self-propelled howitzer entered service with the Russian Army in 1989. While the Russian Army hoped to replace all of its 122mm and 152mm self-propelled artillery with this howitzer, financial constraints mean this replacement is unlikely. At least one 2S19-equipped regiment served in Chechnya as part of VIII Army Corps. MSTA-S comprises a turret mounted on a tracked armoured chassis based on elements of the T-72 and T-80 main battle tanks. The 2S19's gun crew can load the gun at any angle of elevation. Ammunition and gun loading, laying and re-targeting are highly automated, allowing a maximum firing rate of eight rounds per minute with onboard rounds and six or seven rounds per minute with rounds from the ground. The system provides automatic gun loading for projectiles and semi-automatic loading for charges. The design of the ammunition rack allows different types of projectiles to be stored in the same rack, and the automatic loading mechanism can select the type of ammunition and control the loading and the number of rounds. A battery can deliver projectiles on a target and move on to the next firing point before reaction firing. The howitzer's armour gives protection against armour-piercing bullets and projectiles and the 2S19 can also produce a smoke screen.

SPECIFICATIONS

Type:	self-propelled howitzer
Crew:	5
Weight:	42,000kg (92,400lb)
Length (Gun Forward):	11.91m (39.07ft)
Height:	2.98m (9.77ft)
Width:	3.58m (11.74ft)
Ground Clearance:	0.45m (1.47ft)
Vertical Obstacle:	0.5m (1.64ft)
Trench:	2.8m (9.18ft)
Gradient:	47 percent
Powerplant:	V84-A diesel
Power Rating:	840hp
Speed – Maximum:	60km/h (37.5mph)
Cruising Range:	500km (312 miles)
Main Armament:	1 x 152mm
Secondary Armament:	1 x 12.7mm
Ammunition:	50 x 152mm, 300 x 12.7mm

BMD-1

Although originally thought to be a light tank, the BMD is actually the airborne equivalent of the BMP infantry combat vehicle. However, except for the turret and main armament, it is an entirely new design and not a modified BMP. Excluding the obsolescent ASU-57, the BMD was the lightest tracked combat vehicle in the Soviet Red Army. The air-droppable BMD is considerably smaller and lighter than the BMP but has roughly the same capabilities. Its turret armour (maximum 25mm [0.98in]) is thicker than that of the BMP's, but its hull is thinner (maximum 15mm [0.59in]). An internal NBC filtration system provides protection for those inside the vehicle. Two squad members, including the squad leader, ride in the two hatch positions on each side of the driver, while the remaining three occupy the compartment between the turret and engine. The basic BMD was initially introduced around 1970 and within the following three or so years it underwent a variety of minor product-improvement modifications. The final design, designated BMD-1, is most readily identified by a dome-shaped NBC filter intake on the right-centre hull roof. The BMD-1 has retained the protection, mobility and firepower characteristics of the BMD and it can produce a smoke screen if need be.

SPECIFICATIONS

Type:	airborne combat vehicle
Crew:	3 + 3
Weight:	13,300kg (26,600lb)
Length:	6.74m (22.11ft)
Height:	2.15m (7.05ft)
Width:	2.94m (9.64ft)
Ground Clearance:	0.45m (1.47ft)
Vertical Obstacle:	0.8m (2.62ft)
Trench:	1.6m (5.24ft)
Gradient:	60 percent
Powerplant:	diesel
Power Rating:	240hp
Speed – Maximum:	65km/h (40.62mph)
Cruising Range:	600km (375 miles)
Main Armament:	1 x 73mm
Secondary Armament:	2 x 7.62mm, 1 x AT-3 Sagger
Ammunition:	40 x 73mm, 2000 x 7.62mm

BMD-3

The BMD-3 is more rugged than previous BMDs and can be airdropped with its complement of seven men inside the vehicle, enhancing the element of surprise associated with airborne operations. Previously, the crew of other vehicles would be dropped separately, requiring additional time to join up with their fighting vehicle. The all-welded construction of the BMD-3 provides the crew with protection from small-arms fire and shell splinters. The crew consists of commander, gunner, driver and four infantrymen, with the commander normally dismounting with the squad. Three additional infantrymen may be carried in an emergency in the rear. The two-man power-operated turret is armed with a 30mm 2A42 dual-feed cannon and a 7.62mm PKT machine gun mounted coaxially to the right. The roof-mounted ATGM launcher can fire either the AT-4 Spigot or AT-5 Spandrel. The bow-mounted AG-17 30mm automatic grenade launcher and 5.45mm RPKS machine gun are operated by the infantrymen seated in the front of the BMD-3. The automatic grenade launcher has 290 ready rounds and 261 in the rack. The ATGM launcher has 3 ready rounds (one on the launcher), and two stowed. Explosive reactive armour (ERA) is available for use on the BMD-3, but would be a hazard during troop dismounts.

SPECIFICATIONS

Type:	airborne combat vehicle
Crew:	3 + 4
Weight:	12,900kg (28,380lb)
Length:	6m (19.68ft)
Height:	2.25m (7.38ft)
Width:	3.14m (10.3ft)
Ground Clearance:	0.51m (1.67ft)
Vertical Obstacle:	0.8m (2.62ft)
Trench:	2.5m (8.2ft)
Gradient:	60 percent
Powerplant:	2V-06 water-cooled diesel
Power Rating:	450hp
Speed – Maximum:	70km/h (43.75mph)
Cruising Range:	600km (375 miles)
Main Armament:	1 x 30mm
Secondary Armament:	1 x 30mm, 1 x 7.62mm
	1 x 5.45mm, 1 x ATGM

BMP-1

A combination of effective anti-tank firepower, high mobility and adequate protection made the BMP a formidable addition to the inventory of Soviet motorized rifle units. Designed to suit the demands of high-speed offensive in a nuclear war, it carries a 73mm 2A20 gun with maximum rounds of 40 and maximum range of over 2134m (7000ft). The BMP has a three-man crew, including the vehicle commander, who becomes the squad leader when the infantry passengers dismount through the rear exit doors. However, vision blocks and firing ports in the sides and rear of the troop compartment allow the infantrymen to fire assault rifles and light machine guns from inside the vehicle on the move. The troops also carry the RPG-7 or RPG-16 anti-tank grenade launcher and the SA-7/Grail or SA-14 surface-to-air missile, either of which can be fired by a passenger standing in a rear hatch. When sealed in, crew and passengers have NBC protection in the pressurized and filtered hull, which allows them to operate regardless of the outside environment. The BMP is amphibious, propelled through water by its tracks rather than using the water-jet propulsion of the PT-76, and has the range and speed necessary to keep up with the fast-moving tanks it normally follows in offensive formations.

SPECIFICATIONS

Type:	infantry combat vehicle
Crew:	3 + 8
Weight:	13,500kg (44,291lb)
Length:	6.74m (22.11ft)
Height:	2.15m (7.05ft)
Width:	2.94m (9.64ft)
Ground Clearance:	0.39m (1.27ft)
Vertical Obstacle:	0.8m (2.62ft)
Trench:	2.2m (7.21ft)
Gradient:	60 percent
Powerplant:	UTD-20 water-cooled diesel
Power Rating:	300hp
Speed – Maximum:	65km/h (40.62mph)
Cruising Range:	600km (375 miles)
Main Armament:	1 x 73mm
Secondary Armament:	1 x 7.62mm, 1 x Sagger ATGW
Ammunition:	40 x 73mm, 2000 x 7.62mm

BMP-2

The BMP-2 (*Boyevaya Mashina Pyekhota* – Infantry Fighting Vehicle) infantry combat vehicle, fielded in the early 1980s, is an improved version of the BMP-1 incorporating major armament changes. The new two-man turret mounts a 30mm automatic gun with a long thin tube and double-baffle muzzle brake that can be used against aircraft and helicopters. The ATGM launcher on top of the turret can employ either AT-4 Spigot or AT-5 Spandrel missiles, though the AT-5 Spandrel canister is normally mounted. Given the enlarged turret, there are two roof hatches in the rear fighting compartment, rather than the four of the BMP-1, and the BMP-2 accommodates one less passenger. Each side of the troop compartment has three firing ports with associated roof-mounted periscopes. Other options are spall liners, air conditioning and a more powerful engine. An AG-17 30mm automatic grenade launcher modification is offered for the BMP-2, and there is also a drop-in one-man turret, called *Kliver*, with a stabilized 2A72 30mm gun, a four Kornet ATGM launcher, a coaxial 7.62mm machine gun and improved fire control system. The ATGM load consists of one ready on the launcher and four stowed. Thermal sights are available, and the Russian SANOET-1 thermal gunner's sight is available.

SPECIFICATIONS

Type:	infantry combat vehicle
Crew:	3 + 7
Weight:	14,300kg (31,460lb)
Length:	6.72m (22.04ft)
Height:	2.45m (8.03ft)
Width:	3.15m (10.33ft)
Ground Clearance:	0.42m (1.37ft)
Vertical Obstacle:	0.7m (2.29ft)
Trench:	2.5m (8.2ft)
Gradient:	60 percent
Powerplant:	Model UTD-20 6-cylinder diesel
Power Rating:	300hp
Speed – Maximum:	65km/h (40.62mph)
Cruising Range:	600km (375 miles)
Main Armament:	1 x 30mm
Secondary Armament:	1 x 7.62mm, 1 x Spandrel ATGM
Ammunition:	500 x 30mm, 2000 x 7.62mm

BMP-3

The BMP-3 infantry fighting vehicle represents a totally different design concept from the BMP-1 and 2 vehicles, because it is essentially a light tank that can hold a squad of infantry. It has a 100mm main gun that fires high-explosive rounds to demolish buildings, can fire long-range ATGMs through its barrel, and a 30mm autocannon and a medium machine gun as a single unit in the turret. This innovative BMP-3 armament suite has been subjected to criticism in the Russian military, which has focused on deficiencies in the barrel-fired ATGM. The hull of the BMP-3 resembles the BMD airborne infantry fighting vehicle in appearance, with a new turret in the centre of the vehicle. The troop compartment at the rear of the hull is accessed via a pair of doors in the hull rear. The BMP-3 is fully amphibious, propelled in water by two water-jets mounted at the rear of the hull. A drop-in one-man turret called *Kliver* is available, with a stabilized 2A72 30mm gun, a four Kornet ATGM launcher, thermal sights and improved fire control system. Stowed rounds and ATGMs can be passed from the passenger compartment to the gunner for hand loading, including ATGMs. The so-called "HEF"– high-explosive shrapnel – round can be employed in indirect fire mode with air burst up to a range of 7km (4.37 miles).

SPECIFICATIONS

Type:	*infantry fighting vehicle*
Crew:	*3 + 7*
Weight:	*18,700kg (41,140lb)*
Length (Gun Forward):	*7.2m (23.62ft)*
Height:	*2.45m (8.03ft)*
Width:	*3.14m (10.3ft)*
Ground Clearance:	*0.51m (1.67ft)*
Vertical Obstacle:	*0.8m (2.62ft)*
Trench:	*2.5m (8.2ft)*
Gradient:	*60 percent*
Powerplant:	*UTD-29 diesel*
Power Rating:	*500hp*
Speed – Maximum:	*70km/h (43.75mph)*
Cruising Range:	*600km (375 miles)*
Main Armament:	*1 x 100mm*
Secondary Armament:	*1 x 30mm, 3 x 7.62mm*
Ammunition:	*40 x 100mm, 500 x 30mm*

BTR-50P

The BTR-50P is based on the chassis of the PT-76 light amphibious tank with an open-topped troop compartment in the centre. The 20 infantrymen sit on bench seats which run across the full width of the vehicle and enter and leave by climbing over the side of the hull. Armament consists of a pintle-mounted 7.62mm machine gun. The BTR-50P is fully amphibious and propelled in the water by two water-jets at the rear of the hull. It is no longer in production and is being replaced by newer BTRs and BMPs in the Russian Army. However, given the parlous state of Russian finances, this process may take some time. Armoured personnel carriers of the BTR-50P series were issued to the motorized rifle regiment of tank divisions in the Soviet and East German Armies and have also been exported to the Middle East. The BTR-50P, which was first shown in public in November 1957, has undergone a number of modifications. The original BTR-50P had an open-topped fighting compartment, and at first carried no armament. There is now provision, however, for transporting 57mm, 76mm or 85mm guns in the fighting compartment. The guns are loaded onto the vehicle using folding ramps attached to the rear deck. The guns can be fired from the vehicle on land or in the water.

SPECIFICATIONS

Type:	armoured personnel carrier
Crew:	2 + 20
Weight:	14,200kg (31,240lb)
Length:	7.08m (23.22ft)
Height:	1.97m (6.46ft)
Width:	3.14m (10.3ft)
Ground Clearance:	0.37m (1.21ft)
Vertical Obstacle:	1.1m (3.6ft)
Trench:	2.8m (9.18ft)
Gradient:	60 percent
Powerplant:	Model V-6 water-cooled diesel
Power Rating:	240hp
Speed – Maximum:	44km/h (27.5mph)
Cruising Range:	400km (250 miles)
Main Armament:	1 x 7.62mm
Secondary Armament:	none
Ammunition:	1250 x 7.62mm

MT-LB

The MT-LB is an amphibious armoured tracked vehicle with a low-silhouette, box-like hull made of welded steel plates and a small turret on the right front, mounting a single 7.62mm machine gun. Its design is based on the MT-L light transport vehicle and prime mover. The MT-L, which is unarmoured and turretless, was first developed for geological research in the far north of the old Soviet Union. There are four firing ports, one on each side of the vehicle and one in each of the two rear exit doors. Two additional, forward-opening troop exit hatches are located on the flat hull roof. The flat-track suspension consists of six road wheels with no return rollers. The MT-LB can employ an extra-wide track with an "aggressive" grouser to make over snow and swamp operations easier. The MT-LB is a multi-purpose vehicle. For example, when used as a command vehicle it can carry 10 personnel besides its two-man crew (driver and commander-gunner). It is also used as a prime mover for various types of artillery. In this case it can also carry the artillery crew (six to 10 personnel). It is frequently used as prime mover for the T-12 artillery piece. The T-12 is a 100mm smoothbore anti-tank gun mounted on a two-wheeled, split-trail carriage, with a single caster wheel near the trail ends.

SPECIFICATIONS

Type:	multi-purpose tracked vehicle
Crew:	2 + 10
Weight:	11,900kg (26,180lb)
Length:	6.45m (21.16ft)
Height:	1.86m (6.1ft)
Width:	2.86m (9.38ft)
Ground Clearance:	0.4m (1.31ft)
Vertical Obstacle:	0.61m (2ft)
Trench:	2.41m (7.9ft)
Gradient:	60 percent
Powerplant:	YaMZ 238 V, V-8 diesel
Power Rating:	240hp
Speed – Maximum:	61.5km/h (38.43mph)
Cruising Range:	500km (312 miles)
Main Armament:	1 x 7.62mm
Secondary Armament:	none
Ammunition:	2500 x 7.62mm

PT-76

The PT-76 is one of several light amphibious tanks developed and used by the Russian Army. The vehicle entered service in 1954 and is amphibious without additional preparation. Although it is lightly armoured and undergunned for a modern tank, its inherent amphibious capability outweighs these limitations. It carries a 76mm main gun with a maximum effective range of approximately 1500m (4929ft). Operated by a three-man crew, the PT-76 is often used to transport troops. It has a flat, boat-like hull and the suspension has six road wheels and no return rollers. A dish-type turret is mounted over the second, third and fourth road wheels, with a double hatch for commander and loader. The driver's hatch is located beneath the main gun, at the top of the sloping glacis plate. Although it has been replaced in first-line units by the BMP-1 and BMP M1976 vehicles, it may still be found in the reconnaissance companies and battalions of some motorized rifle and tank regiments and divisions, as well as in naval infantry units. Aside from its reconnaissance role, it is also used for crossing water obstacles in the first wave of an attack and for artillery support during the establishment of a beachhead. It is in use in at least 21 countries, including those of the former Warsaw Pact.

SPECIFICATIONS

Type:	*amphibious tank*
Crew:	*3*
Weight:	*14,000kg (30,800lb)*
Length (Gun Forward):	*6.91m (22.67ft)*
Height:	*2.25m (7.38ft)*
Width:	*3.14m (10.3ft)*
Ground Clearance:	*0.51m (1.67ft)*
Vertical Obstacle:	*1.1m (3.6ft)*
Trench:	*2.8m (9.18ft)*
Gradient:	*70 percent*
Powerplant:	*Model V-6B diesel*
Power Rating:	*240hp*
Speed – Maximum:	*44km/h (27.5mph)*
Cruising Range:	*260km (162 miles)*
Main Armament:	*1 x 76mm*
Secondary Armament:	*1 x 7.62mm*
Ammunition:	*40 x 76mm, 1000 x 7.62mm*

SA-13 GOPHER

The Russian SA-13 Gopher mobile surface-to-air missiles (SAM) system is based on an MT LB tracked vehicle. It provides short-range, low-altitude air defence and is replacing the less capable SA-9 system. The SA-13 missile is infrared-guided; the system is equipped with a range-only radar which enables the crew to ensure that the target is within the missile's effective range before firing. Introduced in 1980, it saw combat in Chad and Angola (in both theatres launchers were captured by pro-Western forces and were subsequently supplied to Western intelligence services for analysis). It was also used by Iraq in the Gulf War in 1991. Each vehicle carries four missiles with eight reloads in the cargo compartment. The SA-13 (Strela-10) missile uses an uncooled lead sulphide near-infrared homing type seeker with countermeasures capabilities against infrared decoys. Additionally, it operates in two frequencies to further counter infrared countermeasures. The system can be used against diverse and extremely low-altitude targets as well as in adverse weather. Two variants of the vehicle have been identified. Appraisal of both does not show any significant structural differences, but one carries four HAT BOX passive radars. The launcher vehicle is also capable of firing SA-9 missiles, if required.

SPECIFICATIONS

Type:	self-propelled SAM
Crew:	3
Weight:	12,300kg (27,060lb)
Length:	6.6m (21.65ft)
Height:	3.8m (12.46ft)
Width:	2.85m (9.35ft)
Ground Clearance:	0.4m (1.31ft)
Vertical Obstacle:	0.7m (2.29ft)
Trench:	2.7m (8.85ft)
Gradient:	60 percent
Powerplant:	YaMZ-238V diesel
Power Rating:	240hp
Speed – Maximum:	61.5km/h (38.43mph)
Cruising Range:	500km (312 miles)
Main Armament:	4 x SA-13 SAM
Secondary Armament:	none
Ammunition:	8 x SA-13 SAM

T-64

The T-64, introduced in the late 1960s, was the first of a sophisticated new family of Soviet main battle tanks developed as successors to the T-54/55/62 family. The hull and turret are of cast and welded steel armour incorporating both conventional steel armour and ceramic inserts, which provide superior protection against HEAT rounds. Besides having greatly increased frontal armour protection due to the use of improved layered armour, the T-64 can also attach track protection plates or full-length skirts. Low- flash fuel storage also offers protection to the sides. A front-mounted shovel enables the tank to dig itself in within a few minutes and also increases the armour protection of the lower hull front when it is folded upwards. The 125mm smoothbore main gun fires a hyper-velocity, armour-piercing, fin-stabilized, discarding sabot round believed to have a muzzle velocity of over 1750 metres (5740 feet) per second and an effective range of at least 2000m (6562ft). An automatic loader allows the crew to be reduced to three (commander, gunner and driver), and an automatic spent-cartridge ejection system is employed. The commander is capable of operating all weapons in the tank from his position. The T-64 has an improved, integrated fire control system. It has an onboard computer, and some variants may have a laser rangefinder.

SPECIFICATIONS

Type:	main battle tank
Crew:	3
Weight:	39,500kg (86,900lb)
Length (Gun Forward):	9.2m (30.18ft)
Height:	2.2m (7.21ft)
Width:	3.4m (11.15fft)
Ground Clearance:	0.37m (1.21ft)
Vertical Obstacle:	0.8m (2.62ft)
Trench:	2.28m (7.48ft)
Gradient:	60 percent
Powerplant:	Model 5DTF 5-cylinder diesel
Power Rating:	750hp
Speed – Maximum:	75km/h (46.87mph)
Cruising Range:	400km (250 miles)
Main Armament:	1 x 125 mm
Secondary Armament:	1 x 7.62mm, 1 x 12.7mm
Ammunition:	36 x 125mm, 1250 x 7.62mm

T-72

The T-72, introduced in the early 1970s, is not a further development of the T-64 but rather a parallel design chosen as a high-production tank complementing the T-64 fleet. The T-72 has greater mobility than the T-62, and its V-12 diesel engine has an output of 780hp. This engine appears to be remarkably smoke-free and smooth-running, having eliminated the excessive vibration which was said to cause high crew fatigue in the T-62. The T-72 has better armour protection than the T-62, due to the use of layered armour. The advanced passive armour package of the T-72M and T-72M1 can sustain direct hits from the 105mm gun-equipped M1 Abrams at up to a range of 2000m (6562ft) and survive. The later T-72Ms and T-72M1s are equipped with laser rangefinders ensuring high hit probabilities at ranges of 2000m (6562ft) and below. The 125mm gun common to all the T-72 models is capable of penetrating the M1 Abrams armour at a range of up to 1000m (3281ft). The more recent BK-27 high-explosive, anti-tank (HEAT) round offers a triple-shaped charge warhead and increased penetration against conventional armours and explosive reactive armour (ERA). The BK-29 round, with a hard penetrator in the nose, is designed for use against reactive armour, and also has fragmentation qualities.

SPECIFICATIONS

Type:	main battle tank
Crew:	3
Weight:	44,500kg (97,900lb)
Length (Gun Forward):	9.53m (31.26ft)
Height:	2.22m (7.28ft)
Width:	3.59m (11.77ft)
Ground Clearance:	0.47m (1.54ft)
Vertical Obstacle:	0.85m (2.78ft)
Trench:	2.8m (9.18ft)
Gradient:	60 percent
Powerplant:	V-46 V-12 diesel
Power Rating:	780hp
Speed – Maximum:	60km/h (37.5mph)
Cruising Range:	500km (312 miles)
Main Armament:	1 x 125mm
Secondary Armament:	1 x 7.62mm, 1 x 12.7mm
Ammunition:	45 x 125mm, 2000 x 7.62mm

T-80

The T-80 was the first Soviet operational tank to be powered by a gas turbine engine, with a GTD-1000 gas turbine engine developing 1100hp. The T-80 was also the first production Soviet tank to incorporate a laser rangefinder and ballistic computer system. The original night sight is the II Buran-PA. The 12.7mm machine gun has both remote electronically operated sight PZU-5 and gun-mounted K10-T reflex sight. The day sight can be used at night for launching anti-tank guided missiles (ATGMs) if the target is illuminated. A variety of thermal sights is available, including the Russian Agava-2, French ALIS and Namut sight from Peleng. When fitted with explosive reactive armour (ERA) the T-80 is virtually immune over its frontal arc to penetration from all current NATO ATGMs which rely on a high-explosive, anti-tank (HEAT) warhead to penetrate armour. On the turret of the T-80, the panels are joined to form a shallow chevron pointing. Explosive reactive armour is also fitted to the forward part of the turret roof to provide protection against top-attack weapons. However, the explosive reactive armour does not provide any added protection against armour-piercing, discarding sabot (APDS) or armour-piercing, fin-stabilized, discarding sabot (APFSDS) attack.

SPECIFICATIONS

Type:	main battle tank
Crew:	3
Weight:	46,000kg (101,200lb)
Length (Gun Forward):	9.66m (31.69ft)
Height:	2.2m (7.21ft)
Width:	3.6m (11.81ft)
Ground Clearance:	0.38m (1.24ft)
Vertical Obstacle:	1m (3.28ft)
Trench:	2.85m (9.35ft)
Gradient:	60 percent
Powerplant:	GTD-1000 gas turbine
Power Rating:	1100hp
Speed – Maximum:	70km/h (43.75mph)
Cruising Range:	600km (375 miles)
Main Armament:	1 x 125mm gun/missile launcher
Secondary Armament:	1 x 7.62mm, 1 x 12.7mm
Ammunition:	36 x 125mm, 1250 x 7.62mm

T-84

The T-84 is a Ukrainian upgrade of the T-80UD with a welded turret, a French thermal sight, a more powerful engine, optional use of an Arena active protection system (APS) and SHTORA-1 active infrared ATGM jammer system. The tank fire control system is the 1A42 which includes the 1V517 ballistic computer, two-axis electro-hydraulic weapon stabilizer, rangefinder sight stabilized in two axes as well as a GPK-59 hydro-semicompass azimuth indicator and an azimuth indicator for the turret rotation. This system permits firing on the move. The gunner has the 1G46 day sight and also an infrared sight. The T-80U's gas turbine engine is the GTD-1250 which produces 1250 hp. The GTD-1250 is a three-shaft engine with two cascades of turbo-compression. There is also an independent GTA-18 auxiliary power unit for use when the tank is stationary. The tank has a planetary power transmission with hydraulic servo-system for increased mobility. The track and suspension system is fitted with track and rubber-tyred road wheels, torsion bar suspension with hydraulic telescopic double-acting shock absorbers. The main gun can fire a range of ammunition, including AP (armour-piercing), APDS (armour-piercing, discarding sabot), HEAT (high-explosive, anti-tank) and HE-FRAG (high-explosive fragmentation).

SPECIFICATIONS

Type:	main battle tank
Crew:	3
Weight:	46,000kg (101,200lb)
Length (Gun Forward):	9.66m (31.69ft)
Height:	2.2m (7.21ft)
Width:	3.6m (11.81ft)
Ground Clearance:	0.38m (1.24ft)
Vertical Obstacle:	1m (3.28ft)
Trench:	2.85m (9.35ft)
Gradient:	60 percent
Powerplant:	GTD-1250 gas turbine
Power Rating:	1250hp
Speed – Maximum:	70km/h (43.75mph)
Cruising Range:	600km (375 miles)
Main Armament:	1 x 125mm gun/missile launcher
Secondary Armament:	1 x 7.62mm, 1 x 12.7mm
Ammunition:	36 x 125mm, 1250 x 7.62mm

T-90

The T-90 is the latest development in the T-series of Russian tanks and represents an increase in firepower, mobility and protection. Armament includes one 125mm 2A46M smoothbore gun, stabilized in two axes and fitted with a thermal sleeve. The gun tube can be replaced without dismantling inside the turret, and the gun can fire a variety of ammunition including APDS (armour-piercing, discarding sabot), HEAT (high-explosive, anti-tank), HE-FRAG (high-explosive fragmentation) as well as shrapnel projectiles with time fuses. The T-90S gun can also fire the AT-11 Sniper anti-tank guided missile (ATGM) system. The tank is protected by both conventional armour plating and explosive reactive armour (ERA) and is fitted with the Shtora-1 defensive aids suite. This system includes infrared jammer, laser warning system with four laser warning receivers, grenade discharging system which produces an aerosol screen, and a computerized control system. It is also fitted with NBC (nuclear, biological and chemical) protection equipment. The T-90S has the 1A4GT integrated fire control system, which is automatic but with manual override for the commander. The IFCS contains the gunner's 1A43 day fire control system, gunner's TO1-KO1 thermal imaging sight and commander's PNK-S sight.

SPECIFICATIONS

Type:	main battle tank
Crew:	3
Weight:	46,500kg (102,300lb)
Length (Gun Forward):	9.53m (31.26ft)
Height:	2.2m (7.21ft)
Width:	3.78m (12.4ft)
Ground Clearance:	0.47m (1.54ft)
Vertical Obstacle:	0.8m (2.62ft)
Trench:	2.8m (9.18ft)
Gradient:	60 percent
Powerplant:	V-84MS diesel
Power Rating:	840hp
Speed – Maximum:	unknown
Cruising Range:	500km (312 miles)
Main Armament:	1 x 125mm
Secondary Armament:	1 x 7.62mm, 1 x 12.7mm
Ammunition:	43 x 125mm, 2000 x 7.62mm

TUNGUSKA

Tunguska-M1 is a gun/missile system for low-level air defence. The Tunguska-M1 vehicle carries eight 9M311-M1 surface-to-air missiles. The missile (NATO designation SA-19 Grison) has semi-automatic radar command to line-of-sight guidance, and weighs 40kg (88lb) with a 9kg (19.8lb) warhead. Two twin-barrel 30mm anti-aircraft guns are also mounted on the vehicle. These guns have a maximum firing rate of 5000 rounds per minute and a range of 3000m (9842ft) against air targets. This extends to 4000m (13,123ft) against ground targets. The system has a target acquisition radar and target tracking radar, optical sight, digital computing system, tilt angle measuring system and navigation equipment. Radar detection range is 18km (11.25 miles) and tracking range is 16 km (10 miles). The Tunguska-M1 system is mounted on a tracked vehicle with a multi-fuel engine. It has hydromechanical transmission, hydropneumatic suspension which allows for changing road clearance and hydraulic track-tensioning. The armoured turret has both laying and stabilization drives and power supply. Air-conditioning, heating and filtration systems are also fitted. A Tunguska-M1 battery comprises up to six vehicles and includes a transloader as well as maintenance and training facilities.

SPECIFICATIONS

Type:	self-propelled SAM
Crew:	4
Weight:	34,000kg (74,800lb)
Length:	7.93m (26.01ft)
Height:	4.02m (13.18ft)
Width:	3.24m (10.62ft)
Ground Clearance:	unknown
Vertical Obstacle:	1m (3.28ft)
Trench:	2m (6.56ft)
Gradient:	60 percent
Powerplant:	V-12 turbocharged diesel
Power Rating:	500hp
Speed – Maximum:	65km/h (40.62mph)
Cruising Range:	500km (312 miles)
Main Armament:	4 x 30mm, 8 x SA-19 SAM
Secondary Armament:	none
Ammunition:	1904 x 30mm, 8 x SA-19 SAM

ZSU-23-4 SHILKA

The ZSU-23-4 is a fully integrated, self-propelled anti-aircraft system with four liquid-cooled 23mm automatic cannons mounted on the front of a large, flat, armoured turret. The chassis has many components borrowed from other Soviet armoured vehicles, and the suspension system resembles that of the PT-76 and ASU-85 (six road wheels and no track support rollers). The driver sits in the left front of the hull, and the rest of the crew (commander, gunner and radar operator) is located in the turret. The Gun Dish fire control radar mounted on the rear of the turret can be folded down during travel. The ZSU-23-4 has the capability to both acquire and track low-flying aircraft targets, with an effective anti-aircraft range of 2500m (8202ft). It also is capable of firing on the move because of its integrated radar/gun stabilization system. The high frequency operation of the radar emits a very narrow beam that provides for excellent aircraft tracking while being difficult to detect or evade. However, such a frequency also dictates a limited range, which can be compensated for by linking the system to other long-range acquisition radars in the area. The ZSU-23-4 also can be used against lightly armoured vehicles. The four guns have a cyclic rate of fire of 800–1000 rounds per minute each.

SPECIFICATIONS

Type:	self-propelled anti-aircraft gun
Crew:	4
Weight:	20,500kg (45,100lb)
Length:	6.54m (21.45ft)
Height:	3.8m (12.46ft)
Width:	2.95m (9.67ft)
Ground Clearance:	0.4m (1.31ft)
Vertical Obstacle:	1.1m (3.6ft)
Trench:	2.8m (9.18ft)
Gradient:	60 percent
Powerplant:	Model V-6R diesel
Power Rating:	280hp
Speed – Maximum:	50km/h (31.25mph)
Cruising Range:	450km (281 miles)
Main Armament:	4 x 23mm
Secondary Armament:	none
Ammunition:	2000 x 23mm

TYPE 88K1

The South Korean Type 88K1 main battle tank, which was developed indigenously, is manufactured in Korea by Hyundai Precision using major components from several different countries. Ssangyong Heavy Industries' military diesel engines for the tank are manufactured under licence from MTU of Germany. In May 1996, Hughes Aircraft Company awarded a contract to Kuchera Defence Systems to manufacture electronic assemblies for programmes for the Korean K1 Tank programme. Deliveries of the 105mm K1 to the South Korean Army were completed in 1997. Hyundai has also undertaken the development of the K1 Armoured Recovery Vehicle and Armoured Vehicle Launched Bridge, both based on the K-1 main battle tank. In 1997 Malaysia announced a plan to purchase about 210 tanks worth $730 million US by the end of the century. The first K1A1 tank with the 120mm main armament rolled off the production line at Hyundai on 3 April 1996. The K1A1 features various enhanced functions compared to the existing K1 tanks, including a primary armament of double the penetration power. The new tank's 120mm gun can penetrate vehicles with armour up to 600mm (23.62in) thick, while the old model's 105mm gun could only penetrate up to 300mm (11.81in) of armour.

SPECIFICATIONS

Type:	main battle tank
Crew:	4
Weight:	51,000kg (112,200lb)
Length (Gun Forward):	9.67m (31.72ft)
Height:	2.24m (7.38ft)
Width:	3.59m (11.77ft)
Ground Clearance:	0.46m (1.5ft)
Vertical Obstacle:	1m (3.28ft)
Trench:	2.74m (8.98ft)
Gradient:	60 percent
Powerplant:	MTU MT 871 Ka 501 diesel
Power Rating:	1200hp
Speed – Maximum:	65km/h (40.62mph)
Cruising Range:	500km (312 miles)
Main Armament:	1 x 105mm
Secondary Armament:	1 x 7.62mm, 1 x 12.7mm
Ammunition:	47 x 105mm, 8800 x 7.62mm

ASCOD

This infantry fighting vehicle is operational with the Spanish Army where it is called the *Pizarro*. The vehicle's main armament is a 30mm dual-feed, gas-operated Mauser Mk 30-2 automatic cannon with a 7.62mm coaxial machine gun as a secondary armament. The 30mm gun has a rate of fire of 800 rounds per minute and can fire a range of ammunition including armour-piercing, fin-stabilized, discarding sabot (APFSDS) rounds. The vehicle carries 200 rounds of 30mm and 700 rounds of 7.62mm ammunition ready to fire, and a store of up to 205 rounds of 30mm and up to 2200 rounds of 7.62mm ammunition. The Ascod has a digital ballistic fire control computer, which can be programmed for up to six ammunition types: five for the 30mm gun and one for the machine gun. The gunner's station is equipped with a Kollsman Day Night Range Sight (DNRS), which has a day channel and thermal imaging sight with an integrated laser rangefinder. The 8 to 12 micron thermal imager is dual field of view and has magnifications of times 2.8 and times 8.4. Two sets of three smoke grenade launchers are installed on each side of the turret. Ascod fighting vehicles can be fitted with a laser warning system and NBC (nuclear, biological, chemical) detection system. The Ascod is an excellent infantry fighting vehicle.

SPECIFICATIONS

Type:	*infantry fighting vehicle*
Crew:	*3 + 8*
Weight:	*25,200kg (55,440lb)*
Length:	*6.83m (22.4ft)*
Height:	*2.65m (8.69ft)*
Width:	*3.15m (10.33ft)*
Ground Clearance:	*0.45m (1.47ft)*
Vertical Obstacle:	*0.95m (3.11ft)*
Trench:	*2.3m (7.54ft)*
Gradient:	*75 percent*
Powerplant:	*MTU 8V-183-TE22 8-V90 diesel*
Power Rating:	*600hp*
Speed – Maximum:	*70km/h (43.75mph)*
Cruising Range:	*500km (312 miles)*
Main Armament:	*1 x 30mm*
Secondary Armament:	*1 x 7.62mm*
Ammunition:	*405 x 30mm, 2900 x 7.62mm*

LT 105 LIGHT TANK

The LT 105 Light Tank has been selected by the Royal Thai Marine Corps, which requires 15 tanks plus one command and one recovery vehicle. It is fitted with a three-man turret such as the 105 Low Recoil Force Turret by Otobreda, or the General Dynamics Low Profile Turret. Main armament is a 105mm semi-automatic low recoil tank gun with a 7.62mm coaxial machine gun. The hull and turret are constructed from all-welded steel armour which provides protection against 14.5mm armour-piercing incendiary rounds over the forward 60-degree arc and all-round protection against 7.62mm weapon attack. Additional ballistic protection is available against APFDS (armour-piercing, fin-stabilized, discarding sabot) rounds up to 30mm in diameter fired from a 1000m (3281ft) range over the forward 60-degree arc, and all-round protection against 14.5mm armour-piercing incendiary (API) rounds from a range of 500m (1640ft). Two sets of three smoke grenade launchers are installed on each side of the turret. Ascod fighting vehicles can be fitted with a laser warning system and NBC (nuclear, biological, chemical) detection system. The Ascod is fitted with an MTU 8V-183-TE22 8-V90 diesel engine, rated at 600hp, and a Renk HSWL 106C hydromechanical transmission, plus torsion bar suspension.

SPECIFICATIONS

Type:	light tank
Crew:	4
Weight:	28,500kg (62,700lb)
Length (Gun Forward):	7.63m (25.03ft)
Height:	2.76m (9.05ft)
Width:	3.15m (10.33ft)
Ground Clearance:	0.45m (1.47ft)
Vertical Obstacle:	0.95m (3.11ft)
Trench:	2.3m (7.54ft)
Gradient:	75 percent
Powerplant:	MTU 8V-183-TE22 8-V90 diesel
Power Rating:	600hp
Speed – Maximum:	70km/h (43.75mph)
Cruising Range:	500km (312 miles)
Main Armament:	1 x 105mm
Secondary Armament:	1 x 7.62mm
Ammunition:	40 x 105mm, 4600 x 7.62mm

STRIDSVAGN 122

The Leopard 2 improved 122 is currently the world's most modern main battle tank (MBT). MBT 122, also known as Leopard 2(S), is a further development of the MBT 121 and is partly manufactured in Sweden. It is the most advanced of the Leopard 2 family of tanks. Deliveries of MBT 122 were commenced in 1997 and completed in 2001. A total of 120 MBTs were delivered. The MBT 122 has a crew of four and armament consists of a 120mm smoothbore gun and two 7.62mm machine guns. The vehicle has night-vision sights for both commander and gunner. Types of ammunition include armour-piercing, fin-stabilized, discarding sabot (APFSDS) and HE (high-explosive) rounds. The vehicle has an eye-proof laser and the fire control system allows firing up to ranges of 4km (2.5 miles). The vehicle has an advanced command/control (C2) system, which comprises radio and intercom (Combat Radio, Type RA 180 for speech/computerized data, plus the LTS 90), a technical terminal for the commander, a display unit for the driver, a navigation system (POS 4) and a vehicle computer. The C2 system offers possibilities of presenting a map with tactical information, target designation, logistic and ballistic information, plus navigational data. Information transfer from one vehicle to another is carried out digitally.

SPECIFICATIONS

Type:	main battle tank
Crew:	4
Weight:	62,000kg (136,400lb)
Length (Gun Forward):	9.74m (31.95ft)
Height:	3m (9.84ft)
Width:	3.81m (12.5ft)
Ground Clearance:	0.54m (1.77ft)
Vertical Obstacle:	1.1m (3.6ft)
Trench:	3m (9.84ft)
Gradient:	60 percent
Powerplant:	MTU MB 873 Ka 501
Power Rating:	1500hp
Speed – Maximum:	72km/h (45mph)
Cruising Range:	500km (312 miles)
Main Armament:	1 x 120mm
Secondary Armament:	2 x 7.62mm
Ammunition:	42 x 120mm, 4750 x 7.62mm

AAVP7A1

The AAVP7A1 is an armoured, amphibious fully
tracked landing vehicle. The vehicle carries troops in
water operations from ship to shore, through rough
water and surf zone. It also carries troops to inland objectives after ashore. The primary responsibility of the amphibious assault vehicles (AAVs) during an amphibious operation
is to spearhead a beach assault. Once the AAVs have landed,
they can take on several different tasks: manning check
points, military operations in urban terrain (MOUT) missions, escorting food convoys or mechanized patrol. The
standard AAV comes equipped with a Mk 19 grenade
launcher and a M2 0.5in-calibre machine gun. With a
4545kg (10,000lb) capacity, the AAV can also be used as a
bulk refueler or a field expedient ambulance. It is easily the
most versatile vehicle in the US Marine Corps. When fully
combat loaded, and with a three-man crew, it can carry 25
US Marines. In 1985 the Marine Corps changed the designation of the LVTP7Al to AAVP7A1 – amphibious assault vehicle – representing a shift in emphasis away from the long-
time LVT designation, meaning Landing Vehicle, Tracked.
Without a change of any kind, the AAVP7A1 was to be more
of an armoured personnel carrier and less of a landing vehicle and thus more flexible.

SPECIFICATIONS

Type:	armoured personnel carrier
Crew:	3 + 25
Weight:	27,616kg (60,756lb)
Length:	9.04m (29.65ft)
Height:	2.92m (9.58ft)
Width:	3.56m (11.67ft)
Ground Clearance:	0.45m (1.47ft)
Vertical Obstacle:	0.91m (2.98ft)
Trench:	3.65m (11.97ft)
Gradient:	70 percent
Powerplant:	Cummins VT400 turbocharged
Power Rating:	810hp
Speed – Maximum:	48.28km/h (30.17mph)
Cruising Range:	480km (300 miles)
Main Armament:	1 x 12.7mm
Secondary Armament:	none
Ammunition:	2000 x 12.7mm

M1A1

The M1A1 is an improved version of the M1 main battle tank. It includes a 120mm smoothbore main gun, an NBC (nuclear, biological, chemical) overpressure protection system, and an improved armour package. The primary armour-defeating ammunition of the M256 120mm gun is the armour-piercing, fin-stabilized, discarding sabot (APFSDS) round, which features a depleted uranium penetrator. Depleted uranium has a density two and a half times greater than steel and provides high penetration characteristics. Several other types of ammunition are available as well. The gun is reliable, deadly accurate and has a "hit/kill ratio" that equals or surpasses any tank armament in the world. The turret is fitted with two six-barrelled M250 smoke grenade launchers. The standard smoke grenade contains a phosphorus compound that masks thermal signature of the vehicle to the enemy. The stowage for the main armament ammunition is in armoured ammunition boxes behind sliding armour doors. Armour bulkheads separate the crew compartment from the fuel tanks. The tank is equipped with an automatic Halon fire extinguishing system. This system automatically activates within two milliseconds of either a flash or fire within the tank. The top panels of the tank are designed to blow outwards in the event of penetration by a HEAT projectile.

SPECIFICATIONS

Type:	*main battle tank*
Crew:	*4*
Weight:	*57,141kg (125,710lb)*
Length (Gun Forward):	*9.76m (32.04ft)*
Height:	*2.88m (9.46ft)*
Width:	*3.65m (11.98ft)*
Ground Clearance:	*0.48m (1.58ft)*
Vertical Obstacle:	*1.24m (4.08ft)*
Trench:	*2.74m (9ft)*
Gradient:	*60 percent*
Powerplant:	*AGT-1500 gas turbine*
Power Rating:	*1500hp*
Speed – Maximum:	*72.42km/h (45.26mph)*
Cruising Range:	*440km (275 miles)*
Main Armament:	*1 x 120mm*
Secondary Armament:	*2 x 7.62mm, 1 x 12.7mm*
Ammunition:	*55 x 120mm, 11,400 x 7.62mm*

M1A2

The M1A2 System Enhanced Program (SEP) is an upgrade to the computer core that is the essence of the M1A2 tank. The SEP upgrade includes improved processors, colour and high-resolution flat panel displays, increased memory capacity, user-friendly Soldier Machine Interface (SMI) and an open operating system that will allow for future growth. Major improvements include the integration of the second-generation forward-looking infrared (FLIR) sight, the Under Armor Auxiliary Power Unit (UAAPU) and a Thermal Management System (TMS). The second-generation FLIR is a fully integrated engagement-sighting system designed to provide the gunner and tank commander with significantly improved day and night target acquisition and engagement capability. This system allows 70 percent better acquisition, 15 percent quicker firing and greater accuracy. In addition, a gain of 30 percent greater range for target acquisition and identification will increase lethality and lessen fratricide. The commander's independent thermal viewer provides a hunter/killer capability. The changes are intended to improve lethality, survivability, mobility, sustainability and to provide increased situational awareness and command and control enhancements necessary to supply information to friendly forces.

SPECIFICATIONS

Type:	*main battle tank*
Crew:	*4*
Weight:	*63,072kg (138,758lb)*
Length (Gun Forward):	*9.76m (32.04ft)*
Height:	*2.88m (9.46ft)*
Width:	*3.65m (11.98ft)*
Ground Clearance:	*0.48m (1.58ft)*
Vertical Obstacle:	*1.24m (4.08ft)*
Trench:	*2.74m (9ft)*
Gradient:	*60 percent*
Powerplant:	*AGT-1500 gas turbine*
Power Rating:	*1500hp*
Speed – Maximum:	*72.42km/h (45.26mph)*
Cruising Range:	*424km (265 miles)*
Main Armament:	*1 x 120mm*
Secondary Armament:	*2 x 7.62mm, 1 x 12.7mm*
Ammunition:	*55 x 120mm, 11,400 x 7.62mm*

M2 BRADLEY

The role of the M2 infantry fighting vehicle is to transport infantry on the battlefield, to provide fire cover to dismounted troops and to suppress enemy tanks and fighting vehicles. The M2 carries three crew – commander, gunner and driver – plus six fully equipped infantry men. The main armament is a Boeing 25mm M242 Bushmaster chain gun. The M242 has a single barrel with an integrated dual-feed mechanism and remote feed selection. The gunner can select single or multiple shot mode. The standard rate of fire is 200 rounds per minute but the gun is optionally converted to 500 rounds per minute. An M240C 7.62mm machine gun is mounted coaxially to the right of the Bushmaster. The M2 Bradley is also equipped with the Raytheon tube-launched, optically tracked, wire-guided (TOW) BGM-71 anti-tank missile system. The twin-tube TOW launcher is mounted on the left of the turret. The target is tracked using an optical sight which detects the infrared signal from the back of the missile in flight. A double-wire command link between the missile and the gunner is dispensed from two spools at the back of the missile. The launcher sends flight correction data to the guidance system on the missile via the command link. The range of the TOW missile is 3.75km (2.34 miles).

SPECIFICATIONS

Type:	*infantry fighting vehicle*
Crew:	*3 + 6*
Weight:	*22,727kg (50,000lb)*
Length:	*6.55m (21.48ft)*
Height:	*2.97m (9.74ft)*
Width:	*3.61m (11.84ft)*
Ground Clearance:	*0.43m (1.41ft)*
Vertical Obstacle:	*0.91m (2.98ft)*
Trench:	*2.54m (8.33ft)*
Gradient:	*60 percent*
Powerplant:	*Cummins VTA-903T diesel*
Power Rating:	*500hp*
Speed – Maximum:	*66km/h (41.25mph)*
Cruising Range:	*483km (300 miles)*
Main Armament:	*1 x 25mm*
Secondary Armament:	*1 x 7.62mm, 2 x TOW*
Ammunition:	*900 x 25mm, 2200 x 7.62mm*

M3 BRADLEY

The M3 performs scout missions and carries three crew plus two scouts. The Bradley upgrade programme includes improvements based on operational experience in the 1991 Gulf War. The first low-rate initial production M2A3/M3A3 Bradley was delivered in November 1998 and entered service in April 2000. The system was approved for full-rate production in May 2001 (926 Bradley vehicles are to be upgraded). The US Army has ordered two A3 FIST fire support team vehicles, which can conduct digital fire support coordination, laser designation of targets when stationary and target acquisition when on the move. Upgraded target acquisition, automatic and dual target tracking and automated boresighting are being installed. The gunner is equipped with an integrated sight unit (ISU) which includes a day/thermal sight of magnification times 4 and times 12. An optical relay provides the image of the gunner's sight to the commander. The gunner also has periscopes for forward and side observation. The hull of the Bradley is constructed of welded aluminium and spaced laminate armour. In addition, the M2/M3 Bradleys have appliqué steel armour with provision for additional passive armour or explosive reactive armour (ERA) for increased protection against ballistic weapons on the battlefield.

SPECIFICATIONS

Type:	*infantry fighting vehicle*
Crew:	*3 + 2*
Weight:	*22,727kg (50,000lb)*
Length:	*6.55m (21.48ft)*
Height:	*2.97m (9.74ft)*
Width:	*3.61m (11.84ft)*
Ground Clearance:	*0.43m (1.41ft)*
Vertical Obstacle:	*0.91m (2.98ft)*
Trench:	*2.54m (8.33ft)*
Gradient:	*60 percent*
Powerplant:	*Cummins VTA-903T diesel*
Power Rating:	*500hp*
Speed – Maximum:	*66km/h (41.25mph)*
Cruising Range:	*483km (300 miles)*
Main Armament:	*1 x 25mm*
Secondary Armament:	*1 x 7.62mm, 2 x TOW*
Ammunition:	*900 x 25mm, 2200 x 7.62mm*

M6 BRADLEY LINEBACKER

The Linebacker's combined-arms mission is to provide air defence protection to forward area heavy manoeuvre combat forces, combat support elements, and other critical friendly assets from attack by enemy rotary wing, fixed-wing, unmanned aerial vehicles and cruise missiles. The Bradley Linebacker consists of the M2A2(ODS) Bradley with an integrated, externally mounted launcher that can fire four Stinger missiles while stationary or on the move. An integrated position, navigation and north-seeker capability allows for on-the-move cueing. The standard vehicle-mounted launcher (SVML) carrying four Stinger missiles is added to the 25mm gun turret, eliminating the tube-launched, optically-tracked, wired-guided (TOW) missile which is standard to the Bradley. The 25mm chain gun contributes to the air defence firepower and, as with the 7.62mm machine gun, also provides self-defence. In the event of launcher system damage or failure, or should the manoeuvre force commander choose to employ the Linebacker in a static mode, the system maintains a dismounted Stinger missile capability. Bradley Linebacker retains the capability to maintain pace with the armoured force. Six Stinger missiles are carried internally as ammunition for the external launcher.

SPECIFICATIONS

Type:	air defence vehicle
Crew:	5
Weight:	22,727kg (50,000lb)
Length:	6.55m (21.48ft)
Height:	2.97m (9.74ft)
Width:	3.61m (11.84ft)
Ground Clearance:	0.43m (1.41ft)
Vertical Obstacle:	0.91m (2.98ft)
Trench:	2.54m (8.33ft)
Gradient:	60 percent
Powerplant:	Cummins VTA-903T diesel
Power Rating:	500hp
Speed – Maximum:	66km/h (41.25mph)
Cruising Range:	450km (281 miles)
Main Armament:	1 x 25mm cannon
Secondary Armament:	1 x 7.62mm, 4 x Stinger SAM
Ammunition:	300 x 25mm, 2800 x 7.62mm

M44

Although the M44 155mm Self-propelled Gun has been withdrawn from service with the US Army after seeing service in the Korean and Vietnam Wars, it is still operated by a number of other allied countries, including Turkey. The upgraded M44T system has increased mobility, firepower and reliability. The M44T upgrade package was originally developed in the late 1980s by a German consortium of GLS, MTU and Rheinmetall. The latter company was responsible for the ordnance which is similar to that used on the upgraded M109A3G of the German Army, which in turn is based on that used in the towed FH-70 system. Turkey has modernized its old US-built 155mm M44 guns in a number of key areas, including the installation of a 155mm 39-calibre ordnance and the replacement of the petrol engine by a more fuel-efficient German MTU MB 833 Aa 501 diesel engine developing 450hp, coupled to the original Allison automatic transmission. The original M44 fired a high-explosive projectile to a maximum range of 14.6km (9.12 miles), while the upgraded M44T has a maximum range of 24.7km (15.43 miles) using standard ammunition or 30km (18.75 miles) using enhanced projectiles. The M44 will remain in service around the world well into this century.

SPECIFICATIONS

Type:	self-propelled gun
Crew:	5
Weight:	28,350kg (62,370lb)
Length (Gun Forward):	6.15m (spade up) (20.17ft)
Height:	3.11m (10.2ft)
Width:	3.23m (10.59ft)
Ground Clearance:	0.48m (1.57ft)
Vertical Obstacle:	0.76m (2.49ft)
Trench:	1.82m (5.97ft)
Gradient:	60 percent
Powerplant:	MTU MB 833 Aa 501 diesel
Power Rating:	450hp
Speed – Maximum:	56km/h (35mph)
Cruising Range:	122km (76.25 miles)
Main Armament:	1 x 155mm
Secondary Armament:	1 x 12.7mm
Ammunition:	24 x 155mm, 900 x 12.7mm

M48A5

Developed from the M47 "General Patton" tank, the M48 was the mainstay of the US Army and Marines in Vietnam. Some 11,703 M48s were built between 1952 and 1959. Originally they had 90mm guns, but upon modification to the M48A5 standard they were given the British 105mm. The M48 was withdrawn from US service in favour of the M60, a further development of the M48, but the M48 Patton remains in service around the world. The M48 vehicle is separated into three compartments: the driver's compartment, the fighting compartment and the engine compartment. Above the main gun is a one-million candle-power Xenon searchlight. This light has both a white light and an infrared mode. It is boresighted with the main gun and gunsights so that it can be used to illuminate a target at night. There are a number of variants: M48A5K, South Korean variant with 105mm gun and improved fire control system; M48A5E, Spanish variant with 105mm gun and laser rangefinder; M48A5T1, Turkish upgrade, similar to M48A5; T2 variant includes a thermal sight; CM11, Taiwan variant with a modified M48H turret mated to the M60 hull; CM12, Taiwan variant mates the CM11 turret to the existing M48A3 hull; and M67 flamethrower with a shorter, thicker barrel than the normal 90mm-armed version.

SPECIFICATIONS

Type:	main battle tank
Crew:	4
Weight:	48,089kg (107,595lb)
Length (Gun Forward):	9.29m (30.5ft)
Height:	3.08m (10.1ft)
Width:	3.63m (11.9ft)
Ground Clearance:	0.41m (1.34ft)
Vertical Obstacle:	0.91m (2.98ft)
Trench:	2.59m (8.49ft)
Gradient:	60 percent
Powerplant:	AVDS-1790-2D diesel
Power Rating:	690hp
Speed – Maximum:	48km/h (30mph)
Cruising Range:	413km (258 miles)
Main Armament:	1 x 105mm
Secondary Armament:	1 x 7.62mm, 1 x 12.7mm
Ammunition:	54 x 105mm, 10,000 x 7.62mm

M60

The M60 is one of the world's most successful main battle tanks, with 15,000 having been produced and serving in the armies of 22 countries. The main gun is the 105mm M68 rifled gun with 63 rounds of ammunition. The gun is fully stabilized in the elevation and traverse axes, and is fitted with a thermal sleeve. Both gunner and commander are able to fire the gun and select the type of ammunition to be fired. The coaxial weapon is the 7.62mm M240 machine gun. The tank has two smoke generation systems: an engine exhaust smoke system which sprays fuel into the exhaust manifold, and two six-barrelled smoke grenade launchers which are fitted on ether side of the turret. The tank is fitted with a Raytheon fire control system including an AN/WG-2 eye-safe laser rangefinder and M21 ballistic computer. The gunner's sight is boresighted with the laser rangefinder and the tank's M21 fire control computer senses the type of ammunition which has been selected. The gunner provides the input data for the air temperature and pressure. Other input data is downloaded from various sensors: the target range from the laser rangefinder and cant, crosswind and inertial tracking rates from the gun stabilization unit. This allows accurate engagement against moving targets while the tank is on the move.

SPECIFICATIONS

Type:	main battle tank
Crew:	4
Weight:	52,617kg (115,757lb)
Length (Gun Forward):	9.43m (30.95ft)
Height:	3.27m (10.72ft)
Width:	3.63m (11.9ft)
Ground Clearance:	0.45m (1.47ft)
Vertical Obstacle:	0.91m (2.98ft)
Trench:	2.59m (8.49ft)
Gradient:	60 percent
Powerplant:	AVDS-1790-2C diesel
Power Rating:	750hp
Speed – Maximum:	48km/h (30mph)
Cruising Range:	480km (300 miles)
Main Armament:	1 x 105mm
Secondary Armament:	1 x 7.62mm, 1 x 12.7mm
Ammunition:	63 x 105mm, 7000 x 12.7 & 7.62mm

M109

The 155mm M109 self-propelled medium howitzer is a highly mobile combat support weapon that first saw service in the early 1960s. It has a cruising range of 349km (218 miles) at speeds up to 56.3km/h (35mph). The M109A2/A3/A4 howitzers use the M185 cannon and achieve a range of 23.5km (14.68 miles). The replacement of the 23-calibre barrel with the M284 cannon 39-calibre barrel on the M109A5/A6 increases the range capability to 30km (18.75 miles). The 155mm projectile weighs 44.54kg (98lb). The howitzer is a vehicle that provides armoured combat support, is air transportable, internally loaded, and has excellent ground mobility. It allows firing in a 360-degree circle through its primary armament, the 155mm gun, and its secondary armament, the M2 heavy machine gun. The system is capable of both direct (line of sight) and indirect (out of the line of sight) firing. On 24 May 2000, the government of Egypt requested a possible sale of 279 M109A2/A3 155mm self-propelled howitzers, support equipment, spare and repair parts, publications and technical data, personnel training and training equipment, US government and contractor engineering and logistics personnel services, and other related elements of logistics support. The estimated cost was $48 million US.

SPECIFICATIONS

Type:	self-propelled howitzer
Crew:	6
Weight:	24,948kg (54,886lb)
Length (Gun Forward):	9.12m (29.92ft)
Height:	3m (9.84ft)
Width:	3.15m (10.33ft)
Ground Clearance:	0.45m (1.47ft)
Vertical Obstacle:	0.53m (1.73ft)
Trench:	1.83m (6ft)
Gradient:	60 percent
Powerplant:	Detroit Diesel Model 8V-711
Power Rating:	405hp
Speed – Maximum:	56.3km/h (35mph)
Cruising Range:	349km (218 miles)
Main Armament:	1 x 155mm howitzer
Secondary Armament:	1 x 12.7mm
Ammunition:	36 x 155mm, 500 x 12.7mm

M109A6 PALADIN

The M109A6 Paladin is the latest advancement in 155mm self-propelled artillery. The system enhances previous versions of the M109 by implementing onboard navigational and automatic fire control systems. Paladin has both a Kevlar-lined chassis and a pressurized crew compartment to guard against ballistic, nuclear, biological and chemical threats. The M109A6 is the most technologically advanced cannon in the US Army inventory, has a four-man crew and has a cruising range of 298km (186 miles). The Paladin can operate independently, on the move, it can receive a fire mission, compute firing data, select and take up its firing position, automatically unlock and point its cannon, fire and move out, all with no external technical assistance. Firing the first round from the move in under 60 seconds, a "shoot and scoot" capability protects the crew from counter-battery fire. The M109A6 Paladin is capable of firing up to four rounds per minute to ranges of 30km (18.75 miles). The Paladin features increased survivability characteristics such as day/night operability, NBC (nuclear, biological, chemical) protection with climate control and secure voice and digital communications. The crew remains in the vehicle throughout the mission. The US requirement for these vehicles is estimated to be more than 2000.

SPECIFICATIONS

Type:	*self-propelled gun*
Crew:	*4*
Weight:	*28,909kg (63,600lb)*
Length (Gun Forward):	*9.12m (29.92ft)*
Height:	*3m (9.84ft)*
Width:	*3.15m (10.33ft)*
Ground Clearance:	*0.45m (1.47ft)*
Vertical Obstacle:	*0.53m (1.73ft)*
Trench:	*1.83m (6ft)*
Gradient:	*60 percent*
Powerplant:	*Detroit Diesel DDEC 8V71T*
Power Rating:	*440hp*
Speed – Maximum:	*56.3km/h (35mph)*
Cruising Range:	*298km (186 miles)*
Main Armament:	*1 x 155mm*
Secondary Armament:	*1 x 12.7mm*
Ammunition:	*39 x 155mm, 500 x 12.7mm*

M110A2

The M110A2 is a self-propelled heavy artillery cannon with a crew of 12. Designed to be part of a common family of weapons utilizing the same chassis components, the M107 and M110 were essentially the same vehicle mounting different barrels. This fully tracked, self-propelled artillery weapon fires a 90.9kg (200lb) projectile 203mm (8in) in diameter. The shell leaves the muzzle at a velocity of 700 metres per second (2300 feet per second) and can travel more than 28.8km (18 miles). Ammunition includes standard high explosives, bomblets and high-explosive rockets. The M115 gun has a stepped thread/interrupted screw breechblock, a hydropneumatic variable recoil mechanism and a pneumatic equilibrator. This howitzer system was designed to provide medium-range, general support artillery fire. The M110A2 was built by Bowen-McLauchlin-York of York, Pennsylvania. Widely used in Vietnam, the US Army received this howitzer in 1963 and it served for nearly 30 years. There were 1023 M110A2s in the army inventory in the early 1990s, prior to the system being phased out of service. However, it is still in service with other armies around the world: Belgium, Denmark, Greece, India, Japan, Jordan, South Korea, Spain and Taiwan. It is still deployed with US National Guard units.

SPECIFICATIONS

Type:	self-propelled gun
Crew:	12
Weight:	26,534kg (58,374lb)
Length (Gun Forward):	10.73m (35.2ft)
Height:	3.14m (10.33ft)
Width:	3.14m (10.33ft)
Ground Clearance:	0.44m (1.44ft)
Vertical Obstacle:	1.01m (3.31ft)
Trench:	2.36m (7.74ft)
Gradient:	60 percent
Powerplant:	Detroit Diesel Model 8V-71T
Power Rating:	405hp
Speed – Maximum:	56km/h (35mph)
Cruising Range:	725km (453 miles)
Main Armament:	1 x 203mm
Secondary Armament:	none
Ammunition:	2 x 203mm

M113

The M113 armoured personnel carrier (APC) was the first modern "battle taxi" developed to transport infantry forces on the mechanized battlefield. It is fitted with a two-stroke six-cylinder Detroit diesel providing power through a three-speed automatic gearbox and steering differential. The M113 is built of aircraft-quality aluminum which allows it to possess some of the same strengths as steel at a much lighter weight. This distinct weight advantage allows the M113 to utilize a relatively small engine to power the vehicle, as well as carry a large payload cross-country. Since their initial introduction in 1960, M113-based systems have entered service in more than 50 countries. The systems have been modified into more than 40 identified specific variants, with many times that number of minor field modifications. Many of these modifications have been developed by foreign governments to meet their specific national requirements. Today's M113 fleet includes about 4000 M113A3 vehicles equipped with the most recent recent A3 RISE (Reliability Improvements for Selected Equipment) package. The standard RISE package includes an upgraded propulsion system, greatly improved driver controls (new power brakes and conventional steering controls), external fuel tanks, and 200-amp alternator with four batteries.

SPECIFICATIONS

Type:	armoured personnel carrier
Crew:	2 + 11
Weight:	12,272kg (27,000lb)
Length:	4.86m (15.95ft)
Height:	2.19m (7.2ft)
Width:	2.68m (8.79ft)
Ground Clearance:	0.43m (1.41ft)
Vertical Obstacle:	0.61m (2ft)
Trench:	1.68m (5.51ft)
Gradient:	60 percent
Powerplant:	Detroit Diesel Model 6V-53T
Power Rating:	212hp
Speed – Maximum:	60.7km/h (37mph)
Cruising Range:	480km (300 miles)
Main Armament:	1 x 12.7mm
Secondary Armament:	none
Ammunition:	2000 x 12.7mm

M270 MLRS

The Multiple Launch Rocket System (MLRS) provides an all-weather, indirect area fire weapon system to attack counter-battery, air defence, armoured formations and other high-priority targets at all depths of the tactical battlefield. Primary missions of MLRS include the suppression, neutralization and destruction of threat fire support and forward area air defence targets. The Multiple Launch Rocket System is a versatile weapon system that supplements traditional cannon artillery fire by delivering large volumes of firepower in a short time against critical, time-sensitive targets. MLRS units can use their system's "shoot and scoot" capability to survive while providing fire support for attacking manoeuvre elements. MLRS is not intended to replace cannon artillery, but has been designed to complement it. MLRS consists of a self-loading launcher with an onboard fire control system (FCS). The launcher is mounted on a mobile track vehicle that carries 12 rockets or two Army Tactical Missile System (ATACMS) missiles, which can be fired individually or simultaneously. Rockets have a range beyond 30km (18.75 miles), and the US Army TACMS Block IA missile can reach to 300km (187.5 miles). A conventional barrage of 12 rockets delivers 7728 bomblets or 336 scatterable mines.

SPECIFICATIONS

Type:	multiple rocket launcher
Crew:	3
Weight:	25,000kg (55,000lb)
Length:	6.88m (22.6ft)
Height:	2.57m (8.43ft)
Width:	2.97m (9.75ft)
Ground Clearance:	0.43m (1.41ft)
Vertical Obstacle:	1m (3.28ft)
Trench:	2.29m (7.51ft)
Gradient:	60 percent
Powerplant:	Cummins VTA-903T diesel
Power Rating:	500hp
Speed – Maximum:	64km/h (40mph)
Cruising Range:	483km (302 miles)
Main Armament:	12 x 227mm rockets
Secondary Armament:	none
Ammunition:	none

M270A1 MLRS

The MLRS M270 launcher is being upgraded to accommodate a new MLRS family of munitions, including the US Army Tactical Missile System. The improvements provided by the M270A1 will enhance the field artillery's support to armour and infantry units. They will reinforce the dominant manoeuvre force by improving the corps commander's precision engagement capabilities for shaping the battlefield at extended ranges. The Improved Fire Control System (IFCS) replaces obsolete, maintenance-intensive hardware and software, providing growth potential for future munitions and the possibility of reduced launcher operation and support costs. A Global Positioning System-aided navigation system for the launcher is being developed as part of IFCS to supplement the existing inertial position-navigation system. The Improved Launcher Mechanical System (ILMS) is designed to decrease the time required to aim and load the launcher. This is achieved by providing a faster launcher drive system that moves simultaneously in azimuth and elevation. ILMS is expected to reduce the traverse time from the stowed position to worst case aim point by 80 percent. It will also decrease the mechanical system contribution to reload time by about 40 percent. Reduced launch and reload time will increase survivability.

SPECIFICATIONS

Type:	multiple rocket launcher
Crew:	3
Weight:	25,000kg (55,000lb)
Length:	6.88m (22.6ft)
Height:	2.57m (8.43ft)
Width:	2.97m (9.75ft)
Ground Clearance:	0.43m (1.41ft)
Vertical Obstacle:	1m (3.28ft)
Trench:	2.29m (7.51ft)
Gradient:	60 percent
Powerplant:	Cummings VTA-903T diesel
Power Rating:	500hp
Speed – Maximum:	64km/h (40mph)
Cruising Range:	483km (302 miles)
Main Armament:	12 x 227mm rockets
Secondary Armament:	none
Ammunition:	none

M551 SHERIDAN

The M551 Sheridan was developed to provide the US Army with a light armoured reconnaissance vehicle with heavy firepower. The main armament consists of an 152mm M81 gun/missile launcher capable of firing conventional ammunition and the MGM-51 Shillelagh anti-tank missile. Due to problems with the gun-tube-launched anti-tank missile, the Sheridan was not fielded widely throughout the army. The gun would foul with caseless ammunition, gun firing would interfere with missile electronics, and the entire vehicle recoiled with unusual vigour when the gun was fired, since the 152mm gun was too big for the lightweight chassis. The Shillelagh missiles were evidently never used in anger. In addition to the main gun/missile launcher, the M551 is armed with a 7.62mm M240 machine gun and a 12.7mm M2 anti-aircraft machine gun. Protection for the four-man crew is provided by an aluminum hull and steel turret. Although light enough to be airdropped, the aluminum armour is thin enough to be pierced by heavy machine-gun rounds, and the vehicle is particularly vulnerable to mines. As projectile technology advanced, the Sheridan's potential declined and it was phased out of the US inventory beginning in 1978. However, the M551 is still used by the 82nd Airborne Division.

SPECIFICATIONS

Type:	light tank
Crew:	4
Weight:	15,830kg (34,826lb)
Length:	6.79m (22.3ft)
Height:	2.94m (9.64ft)
Width:	4.11m (13.5ft)
Ground Clearance:	0.48m (1.57ft)
Vertical Obstacle:	0.83m (2.62ft)
Trench:	2.54m (8.3ft)
Gradient:	60 percent
Powerplant:	Detroit Diesel Model 6V-53T
Power Rating:	300hp
Speed – Maximum:	70km/h (43.75mph)
Cruising Range:	600km (375 miles)
Main Armament:	1 x 152mm
Secondary Armament:	1 x 7.62mm, 1 x 12.7mm
Ammunition:	20 x 152mm, 3080 x 7.62mm

M730 CHAPARRAL

Thislightweight carrier is a product improved version of the M730A1 that is used to transport the improved (and heavier) M54A2 Chaparral Aerial Intercept Guided Missile pallet. The vehicle incorporates the Reliability Improvement for Selected Equipment (RISE) power package and a nuclear, biological, chemical (NBC) collective protection system. The M730A2 was the first M113 derivative to use the RISE package. Approximately 500 M730A1 systems were converted to M730A2 RISE during the period 1988–93 at three depot locations. Fieldings were completed in the third quarter of 1993. Residual conversion kits are being used to support M548A1 to M548A3 conversions. The Chaparral missile provides mobile short-range air defence to defeat low-altitude aircraft. The system is designed to be mobile, self-contained and air transportable. The M730 is a mobile light air defence system with a turret mounted on a tracked vehicle carrying four ready-to-fire missiles; the Chaparral is a ground-launched version of the air-to-air Sidewinder. Chaparral consists of infrared heat-seeking missiles, a launcher with a forward-looking infrared (FLIR) sight, and a tracked vehicle. Chaparral provides the US Army with point defence of vital corps areas against direct enemy air attack.

SPECIFICATIONS

Type:	*self-propelled SAM*
Crew:	*4*
Weight:	*11,909kg (26,200lb)*
Length:	*6.04m (19.83ft)*
Height:	*2.89m (9.43ft)*
Width:	*2.68m (8.79ft)*
Ground Clearance:	*0.43m (1.41ft)*
Vertical Obstacle:	*0.61m (2ft)*
Trench:	*1.68m (5.51ft)*
Gradient:	*60 percent*
Powerplant:	*Detroit Diesel Model 6V-53*
Power Rating:	*212hp*
Speed – Maximum:	*60km/h (37.5mph)*
Cruising Range:	*480km (300 miles)*
Main Armament:	*4 x Chaparral SAM*
Secondary Armament:	*none*
Ammunition:	*12 x Chaparral SAM*

M901A3

The M901A3 Improved TOW Vehicle (ITV) is a weapon system using TOW components mounted on a modified M113A3. It incorporates the RISE power-pack and improved driver controls. The TOW components are mounted in a launcher platform that is attached to a modified M27 cupola. An elevating mechanism positions the launcher platform into reload and elevated positions. The system is capable of firing two missiles without reloading and carries 10 TOW rounds in the missile rack. The BGM-71 TOW wire-guided heavy anti-tank missile is used in anti-armour, anti-bunker, anti-fortification and anti-amphibious landing roles. The missile has command to line-of-sight guidance. The weapons operator uses a telescopic sight to view a point on the target and then fires the missile. The missile has a two-stage solid propellant rocket motor. Guidance signals from the guidance computer are transmitted along two wires, which spool from the back of the missile to the control system on the missile. The CACS-2 control system uses differential piston-type actuators. For penetration of tanks protected with explosive reactive armour (ERA), TOW 2A is equipped with a tandem warhead. A small disrupter charge detonates the reactive armour and allows the main shaped charge to penetrate the main armour.

SPECIFICATIONS

Type:	armoured TOW carrier
Crew:	4
Weight:	11,794kg (25,947lb)
Length:	4.83m (15.84ft)
Height:	3.35m (11ft)
Width:	2.68m (8.79ft)
Ground Clearance:	0.43m (1.41ft)
Vertical Obstacle:	0.61m (2ft)
Trench:	1.68m (5.51ft)
Gradient:	60 percent
Powerplant:	Detroit Diesel Model 6V-53T
Power Rating:	215hp
Speed – Maximum:	67km/h (41.87mph)
Cruising Range:	483km (302 miles)
Main Armament:	1 x twin TOW ATGW launcher
Secondary Armament:	1 x 7.62mm
Ammunition:	2 + 10 TOW, 1000 x 7.62mm

M981 FISTV

The M981 Fire Support Team Vehicle (FISTV) is used as an artillery forward observer vehicle in accordance with the US fire support team concept. Its primary mission is to enhance combined arms efficiency by providing the FIST headquarters with an operating base for targeting, self-locating and designating equipment which will provide improvements in first-round accuracy and by providing mobility and survivability comparable with the manoeuvre units being supported. The weapons station on the M981 contains the AN/TVQ-2 ground and vehicle laser locator designator with north-finding module and line-of-sight sub-system, land navigation system and extensive communications equipment. The turret of the M981 is designed to mimic that of the M901, thus making the vehicle less conspicuous to enemies. The M981 incorporates the armoured external fuel tank system for increased stowage capability and increased crew survivability. The first conversions from M113A2 chassis began in 1983 and the first production vehicles appeared in December 1984. The US Army has a total requirement for 967 FISTVs. First deliveries to US units were made in 1985 and deployments were completed in 1990. The FISTV fitted with the RISE power package is designated the M981A3.

SPECIFICATIONS

Type:	artillery observation vehicle
Crew:	4
Weight:	11,794kg (25,947lb)
Length:	4.83m (15.84ft)
Height:	3.35m (11ft)
Width:	2.68m (8.79ft)
Ground Clearance:	0.43m (1.41ft)
Vertical Obstacle:	0.61m (2ft)
Trench:	1.68m (5.51ft)
Gradient:	60 percent
Powerplant:	Detroit Diesel Model 6V-53T
Power Rating:	215hp
Speed – Maximum:	67km/h (41.87mph)
Cruising Range:	483km (302 miles)
Main Armament:	1 x twin TOW ATGW launcher
Secondary Armament:	1 x 7.62mm
Ammunition:	2 + 10 TOW, 1000 x 7.62mm

M1064A3

The M1064A3 is a member of the M113A3 vehicle family developed and produced by FMC Corporation. Power is supplied by a 275hp Detroit Diesel Model 6V53T turbocharged diesel engine driving through an Allison X200-4 (cross-drive) transmission. The M1064A3 incorporates all of the mobility and reliability improvements of the M113A3 vehicle, including powertrain, engine diagnostics, driver's station, and electrical system. Survivability is enhanced through the use of external fuel tanks. The M1064A3 has the same silhouette as the M113A3 armoured personnel carrier and features a welded-in cross beam, additional floor support structures to withstand mortar reaction forces, and an enlarged three-piece top firing hatch. The 120mm weapon has a 90-degree traverse for firing over the rear of the vehicle. The M106 107mm mortar carrier has a 4.2in (107mm) M30 mortar mounted on a turntable in the rear which fires through a large hatch in the roof. The baseplate for the mortar is mounted externally on the left side of the vehicle for use when firing the mortar dismounted. However, as can be seen from the photograph, the crew is vulnerable to small-arms fire. The M125 vehicle is of similar design, carrying a 81mm mortar. Kits to convert M106 and M125 vehicles to the M1064A3 configuration are available.

SPECIFICATIONS

Type:	self-propelled mortar
Crew:	6
Weight:	12,809kg (28,240lb)
Length:	4.86m (15.94ft)
Height:	2.31m (7.57ft)
Width:	2.68m (8.79ft)
Ground Clearance:	0.43m (1.41ft)
Vertical Obstacle:	0.61m (2ft)
Trench:	1.68m (5.51ft)
Gradient:	60 percent
Powerplant:	Detroit Diesel Model 6V53T
Power Rating:	275hp
Speed – Maximum:	66km/h (41mph)
Cruising Range:	480km (300 miles)
Main Armament:	1 x 120mm mortar
Secondary Armament:	1 x 12.7mm
Ammunition:	69 x 120mm, 2000 x 12.7mm

M2001 CRUSADER

The Crusader self-propelled howitzer is a replacement for the Paladin and the US Army requirement is expected to be for over 800 vehicles, entry into service beginning in 2008. Crusader provides enhanced survivability, lethality and mobility and is more easily deployable and sustainable than current systems. A battery of six Crusaders can deliver 15,000kg (33,000lb) of ammunition in less than five minutes. Crusader consists of two vehicles, the M2001 155mm self-propelled howitzer and the M2002 armoured re-supply vehicle. The 155mm self-propelled howitzer has fully automated ammunition handling and firing that allows firing of the 39 onboard rounds at rates of up to 10 rounds per minute to ranges in excess of 40km (25 miles). The first rounds of a mission can be fired in 15 to 30 seconds. Additionally, one Crusader vehicle can fire up to eight rounds to strike a single target at the same time. The digital fire control system calculates separate firing solutions for each of the eight projectiles. Crusader is re-supplied by the M2002 ammunition re-supply vehicle, which is equipped with a fully automated ammunition handling subsystem. This allows its three-man re-supply crew to automatically transfer, under armour, up to 48 rounds of ammunition and fuel in less than 12 minutes.

SPECIFICATIONS

Type:	self-propelled howitzer
Crew:	3
Weight:	36,100kg (79,420lb)
Length (Gun Forward):	12.89m (42.3ft)
Height:	2.89m (9.5ft)
Width:	3.5m (11.5ft)
Ground Clearance:	0.43m (1.43ft)
Vertical Obstacle:	0.79m (2.6ft)
Trench:	0.82m (2.7ft)
Gradient:	60 percent
Powerplant:	Honeywell LV100-5
Power Rating:	440hp
Speed – Maximum:	67.2km/h (42mph)
Cruising Range:	402km (251 miles)
Main Armament:	1 x 155mm
Secondary Armament:	1 x 12.7mm
Ammunition:	39 x 155, 500 x 12.7mm

MK154

The MK154 Launcher, Mine Clearance (LMC) is part of the Mark 1 Mine Clearance System which also includes three M59 Linear Demolition Charges (LDCs), three MK22 Mod 3/4 Rockets and an AAVP7A1 vehicle. Its role is to breach a lane through a minefield during an amphibious assault and subsequent operations inland. The MK154 LMC can deploy three linear demolition chargers from the water or land. Each linear demolition charge is 100m (328ft) long and will be the initial minefield breaching asset used. Because the LDC is only effective against single impulse, non-blast resistant, pressure-fused mines, a mechanical proofing device must also be used in a lane that has been explosively breached. The MK154 LMC is an electric and hydraulic system which can be installed into any AAVP7A1. All of the hydraulics are self-contained, and the electrical power is provided through the host vehicle slave receptacle. The system has the capability to house and fire three LDCs using three MK22 Rockets. The overpressure created by each of the LDCs will clear a path 16m (52.49ft) wide and 100m (328ft) long through a minefield. The width of the lane and the ability to neutralize mines is dependent upon the mine type and fusing. The MK154 is a valuable asset to the US Marine Corps.

SPECIFICATIONS

Type:	*mine clearer*
Crew:	*3*
Weight:	*37,442kg (82,372lb)*
Length:	*9.04m (29.65ft)*
Height:	*2.92m (9.58ft)*
Width:	*3.56m (11.67ft)*
Ground Clearance:	*0.45m (1.47ft)*
Vertical Obstacle:	*0.91m (2.98ft)*
Trench:	*3.65m (11.97ft)*
Gradient:	*70 percent*
Powerplant:	*Continental LV-1790-1 petrol*
Power Rating:	*810hp*
Speed – Maximum:	*48km/h (30mph)*
Cruising Range:	*480km (300 miles)*
Main Armament:	*1 x 7.62mm*
Secondary Armament:	*none*
Ammunition:	*2000 x 7.62mm*

STINGRAY

SPECIFICATIONS

The Stingray light tank was developed to fill requirements for a light tank with increased strategic and tactical mobility and main battle tank firepower. It was developed with the export market in mind. For example, it fires all NATO 105mm ammunition, as well as British and US armour-piercing, fin-stabilized, discarding sabot (APFSDS) rounds. Stingray can climb 60-percent gradients, and traverses 2.7ft (822mm) vertical obstacles and water depths to 3.5ft (1066mm). The Stingray is the only light tank mounting the NATO 105mm cannon currently in production. Textron Marine & Land Systems has now completed an advanced version of the Stingray, known as Stingray II, which has increased ballistic protection and improved fire control, and is expected to have wide appeal to many international customers. The tank's sensors include an M36E1 SIE day/night sight with laser rangefinder for gunner and optional thermal sight, seven periscopes for commander with optional NV52 day/night sight, and an optional digital fire control system. The tank can be fitted with a nuclear, biological, chemical (NBC) protection system. Other defensive measures include two four-shot smoke grenade dischargers. Secondary armament consists of either two 7.62mm machine guns or one 7.62mm and one 12.7mm.

Type:	light tank
Crew:	4
Weight:	21,205kg (46,651lb)
Length (Gun Forward):	9.30m (30.51ft)
Height:	2.55m (8.36ft)
Width:	2.71m (8.89ft)
Ground Clearance:	0.46m (1.56ft)
Vertical Obstacle:	0.82m (2.7ft)
Trench:	2.13m (6.98ft)
Gradient:	60 percent
Powerplant:	Detroit Diesel Model 8V-92TA
Power Rating:	535hp
Speed – Maximum:	67km/h (42mph)
Cruising Range:	483km (302 miles)
Main Armament:	1 x 105mm
Secondary Armament:	2 x 7.62mm
Ammunition:	32 x 105mm, 2800 x 7.62mm

40.10 WM

The Iveco range of light vehicles was designed for high mobility both on and off road, which makes them ideal for military use. As such, they fill the gap between traditional jeeps and medium trucks. Like many modern utility vehicles, they have been designed for the easy and simple installation of different body types. The heart of the 40.10 is a high-power diesel engine, either a turbocharged model developing 103 horsepower or a turbocharged aftercooled version developing 122 horsepower. Use on rough terrain is made easier by the front independent suspension, while the large tyres allow the vehicle to operate in mud, sand or snow. The large radiator cools the engine even in tropical temperatures, while a large and efficient air cleaner ensures suitable filtration in desert conditions. When operating in cold climates, the ambulance can be fitted with a supplementary heater to pre-heat the engine before starting at low temperatures. The body of the cab consists of a steel shell, on the sides of which are fitted fastened panels in glass-reinforced resin. The cab itself can be covered by a tarpaulin or a hard top, and the windscreen can be tilted forward to reduce height to facilitate loading the truck on an aircraft or for parachute drops. A normal ambulance payload is four stretchers.

SPECIFICATIONS

Type:	ambulance
Manufacturer:	Iveco
Powerplant:	Fiat 8142 diesel
Horsepower:	103
Transmission:	5 + 5
Length:	5.5m (18.04ft)
Width:	2m (6.56ft)
Height:	2.86m (9.38ft)
Weight:	4500kg (9900lb)
Ground clearance:	0.4m (1.31ft)
Armament:	none
Crew:	2
Top speed:	100km/h (62.5mph)
Range:	600km (375 miles)
Fording:	0.5m (1.64ft)
Gradient:	60 percent
Configuration:	4 x 4

LAND ROVER

The Land Rover Battlefield Ambulance, based on the TUM chassis, replaced the British Army's fleet of wheeled battlefield ambulances between 1997 and 1999. It has a capacity for a combination of up to four stretcher cases or six seated casualties and provides a very high standard of medical facilities. It is airportable and meets amphibious requirements, making it suitable for rapid deployment to anywhere in the world. There have been three generations of British Army Land Rover ambulances. The First Generation utilized an extended and raised body on either a Series II/IIA or, less commonly, Series III 109in chassis. These were in production from the late 1950s right up to the early 1980s. The Second Generation was based on a rebuilt 101 Forward Control model and had a comparatively short production run. All 101-based ambulances were built between 1981 and 1982 using factory re-manufactured 1976 vehicles, 101FC production having ceased in 1978. The current version, the Third Generation, is based on the military-specified Defender XD130 (and, in this guise, is also known as "Pulse" or, less accurately, "Wolf"). Like all Land Rovers, this model is rugged and can be serviced in the field if need be, and the tools required for this servicing are often just a hammer and a few spanners.

SPECIFICATIONS

Type:	ambulance
Manufacturer:	Land Rover
Powerplant:	300 TDI diesel
Horsepower:	85
Transmission:	5 + 1
Length:	3.72m (12.2ft)
Width:	1.79m (5.87ft)
Height:	1.99m (6.52ft)
Weight:	3700kg (8140lb)
Ground clearance:	0.21m (0.68ft)
Armament:	none
Crew:	3
Top speed:	140km/h (87.5mph)
Range:	500km (312 miles)
Fording:	0.5m (1.64ft)
Gradient:	70 percent
Configuration:	4 x 4

FV 432

First introduced in 1962, the FV series of armoured vehicles was developed to fulfil no less than 14 roles including command post armoured personnel carrier, ambulance, minelayer, recovery and repair vehicle, mortar carrier, radar or troop carrier. Totally nuclear, biological, chemical (NBC) proof, it can carry up to 10 men and 2 crew and may be armed with a 7.62mm machine gun or turret-mounted L37 machine gun. This ubiquitous vehicle fulfils a number of roles for the British Army, including armoured command post, 81mm mortar carrier, artillery observation post, field artillery computer equipment carrier, minelayer, Cymbeline radar carrier, basic troop carrier and ambulance. Each brigade in the British Army has a field ambulance unit that operates in direct support of battle groups. The field ambulance units provide dressing stations where casualties are treated prior to transfer to a field hospital. Vehicles such as the FV 432 provide the field ambulance units with integral ambulance support on the battlefield, which also includes wheeled vehicles. The care of the sick and wounded is the responsibility of the Royal Army Medical Corps, whose personnel in peacetime are based at the various medical installations throughout the world or in field force units.

SPECIFICATIONS

Type:	ambulance
Manufacturer:	GNK Sankey
Powerplant:	Rolls-Royce K60 diesel
Horsepower:	240hp
Transmission:	6 + 1
Length:	5.25m (17.22ft)
Width:	2.8m (9.18ft)
Height:	2.28m (7.48ft)
Weight:	15,280kg (33,616lb)
Ground clearance:	0.5m (1.64ft)
Armament:	none
Crew:	2
Top speed:	52km/h (32.5mph)
Range:	580km (362 miles)
Fording:	1m (3.28ft)
Gradient:	60 percent
Configuration:	tracked

M997

The M996, M996A1, M997, M997A1, M1035 and M1035A1 High Mobility Multipurpose Wheeled Vehicles (HMMWVs) are the ambulance configuration of the HMMWV family. The vehicles are equipped with basic armour and used to transport casualties from the battlefield to the medical aid stations. The HMMWV's mission is to provide a light tactical vehicle for command and control, special purpose shelter carriers, and special purpose weapons platforms throughout all areas of the modern battlefield. It is supported using the current logistics and maintenance structure established for army wheeled vehicles. The M996/M996A1 are designated as mini-ambulances and can transport up to two litter patients, six ambulatory patients or a combination of litter and ambulatory patients. The M997/M997A1 are designated as maxi-ambulances and can transport up to four litter patients, eight ambulatory patients or a combination of litter and ambulatory patients. The M1035/M1035A1 are soft-top ambulances and can transport up to two litter patients. The vehicles can climb 60 percent slopes and traverse a side slope of up to 40 percent fully loaded. These configurations of the HMMWV are not equipped with the self-recovery winch.

SPECIFICATIONS

Type:	ambulance
Manufacturer:	AM General
Powerplant:	General Motors diesel
Horsepower:	150hp
Transmission:	3 + 1
Length:	5.13m (16.83ft)
Width:	2.15m (7.08ft)
Height:	2.59m (8.5ft)
Weight:	4136kg (9100lb)
Ground clearance:	0.4m (1.31ft)
Armament:	none
Crew:	2
Top speed:	88km/h (55mph)
Range:	539km (337 miles)
Fording:	0.76m (2.5ft)
Gradient:	60 percent
Configuration:	4 x 4

SAMARITAN

The Samaritan is one of the Scorpion family of reconnaissance vehicles, equipped to fulfil the fire support role with a 76mm gun, but also capable of fulfiling to a large degree the anti-tank and reconnaissance roles. The greatly increased mobility afforded by tracks, combined with advanced production techniques, permitted the design of a light, powerful, tracked reconnaissance weapon system with a fire power hitherto unattainable at the weight desired. Costs throughout have been kept down to the minimum, consistent with attaining the objects of mobility, firepower and protection. This has been done by using common components and layout and by using only assemblies and techniques known to be proven. At the same time the most modern materials and methods have been employed. The emphasis throughout has been on simplicity, simplicity in ease of maintenance and in crew training. Similarly inherent reliability has been built in. However, the basic vehicles are capable of sophistication tasks according to the user's requirements by adding optional equipment such as night-fighting aids, radar and gas detector systems. The Samaritan can accommodate up to six stretchers in the rear compartment, and can be fitted into the fuselage of a C-130 Hercules transport aircraft.

SPECIFICATIONS

Type:	ambulance
Manufacturer:	Alvis
Powerplant:	Jaguar 4.2 litre
Horsepower:	190
Transmission:	7 + 7
Length:	5.07m (16.63ft)
Width:	2.24m (7.34ft)
Height:	2.42m (7.93ft)
Weight:	8660kg (19,052lb)
Ground clearance:	0.35m (1.14ft)
Armament:	none
Crew:	2
Top speed:	72.5km/h (45.31mph)
Range:	483km (302 miles)
Fording:	1.06m (3.47ft)
Gradient:	60 percent
Configuration:	tracked

AVLB

The Armoured Vehicle Launcher Bridge (AVLB) launches a single Close Support Bridge to cross gaps of up to 24.5m (80.38ft) or a combination of such bridges to cross gaps of up to 60m (196.85ft). A single bridge can be laid in about three minutes without exposing the crew to enemy fire. Once the bridge has been laid, the launch vehicle can drive over it and recover it from the far bank. The hull of the AVLB is similar to that of the Chieftain main battle tank, with the driver seated at the front of the hull and the commander and radio operator being behind the driver. The suspension consists of three bogies per side, each bogie having two sets of road wheels and a set of three horizontal springs. The first and last road wheel stations have a hydraulic shock absorber. The bridge girders and launching structure are made of high-strength nickel-alloy steel to facilitate the bearing of armoured fighting vehicles. The bridge is made of two tracks, and each track is capable of bearing the load of light armoured vehicles, thus allowing two-way traffic with vehicles of this size. Each Chieftain bridgelayer usually has one No 8 and one No 9 tank bridge, one carried on the vehicle and the other on a specially adapted Scammel prime mover towing a semi-trailer. The production total for the British Army was 37.

SPECIFICATIONS

Type:	*bridging vehicle*
Manufacturer:	*Vickers Defence Systems*
Powerplant:	*L60 multifuel*
Horsepower:	*730*
Transmission:	*6 + 2*
Length:	*13.74m (45.07ft)*
Width:	*4.16m (13.64ft)*
Height:	*3.92m (12.86ft)*
Weight:	*53,300kg (117.260lb)*
Ground clearance:	*0.5m (1.64ft)*
Armament:	*2 x 7.62mm*
Crew:	*3*
Top speed:	*42km/h (26.25mph)*
Range:	*400km (250 miles)*
Fording:	*1.06m (3.47ft)*
Gradient:	*60 percent*
Configuration:	*tracked*

AVLB

The 26m- (85.3ft-) long MLC 70 LEGUAN Armoured Vehicle Launcher Bridge (AVLB) produced in Germany can be launched from a number of tank chassis, including the following: the American M1A1/A2 "Wolverine" Heavy Assault Bridge (HAB), the German Leopard 1 and the American M60. The bridge itself has been designed for the modern battlefield and possesses the following qualities: bridge laying in less than five minutes, fully automatic launching through an electronically controlled bridge laying system, one-man operation from within the vehicle and with hatch closed, the remote control of a bridge-laying operation via cable connection (when visibility is obstructed at the constructing site), and bridge laying/retrieval in darkness. The bridge can even be modified to act as a ferry for the crossing of very wide waterways. The bridge is placed by the bridgelaying vehicle or tank on pontoons for this application. Hydraulically adjusted ramps are added at the ends of the bridge to make it easier to drive on and off the ferry. The aluminium pontoons feature an integrated pump-jet drive which makes them highly manoeuvrable, permitting movements in shallow water. Continuous crossing of vehicles and equipment is enabled by coupling the individual ferries together so that they form a floating bridge.

SPECIFICATIONS

Type:	bridging system
Manufacturer:	MAN Technologie AG
Powerplant:	MB 873 Ka-501 multifuel
Horsepower:	830
Transmission:	4 + 2
Length:	13.37m (43.86ft)
Width:	4m (13.12ft)
Height:	3.85m (12.63ft)
Weight:	50,000kg (110,000lb)
Ground clearance:	0.42m (1.37ft)
Armament:	none
Crew:	2
Top speed:	62km/h (38.75mph)
Range:	450km (281 miles)
Fording:	1.2m (3.93ft)
Gradient:	60 percent
Configuration:	tracked

BIBER

The Leopard 1-based Armoured Bridgelayer Biber, with a crew of two men, is equipped with a hydraulic bridge system which is laid horizontally (the so-called cantilever principle). This means that it can be used without the disadvantage of being observed some distance away by the enemy. It is operated by the driver via the central hydraulic system and can be laid under armour protection within approximately three minutes, even in the range of enemy small arms. The laying procedure is divided into several stages that are controlled by a sequence control system. The picking up of the bridge can be done either by its own vehicle or another Biber from either side of the defile, by proceeding in reverse sequence. Offering an effective support length of 20m (65.61ft), the Biber bridge consists of two 11m (36.08ft) bridge sections, mounted in two pairs, one above the other on both sides on top of the vehicle in transport mode. The hull of the Biber is almost identical to that of the Leopard 1 main battle tank, with the driver seated at the front of the hull on the right side and the commander in the centre (the engine and transmission are mounted at the rear). The torsion bar suspension consists of seven road wheels with the drive sprocket at the rear and the idler at the front.

SPECIFICATIONS

Type:	bridging system
Manufacturer:	Rheinmetall
Powerplant:	MB 873 Ka-501 multifuel
Horsepower:	830
Transmission:	4 + 2
Length:	11.79m (38.68ft)
Width:	4m (13.12ft)
Height:	3.55m (11.64ft)
Weight:	45,300kg (99,660lb)
Ground clearance:	0.42m (1.37ft)
Armament:	none
Crew:	2
Top speed:	62km/h (38.75mph)
Range:	450km (281 miles)
Fording:	1.2m (3.93ft)
Gradient:	60 percent
Configuration:	tracked

M3 AMPHIBIOUS RIG

The M3 amphibious bridging and ferry system currently in service with the British Army is a replacement for the earlier M2 system. Improvements include the ability to be driven on land and water from the same end. The four-man crew sit in the cab in the front of the vehicle. Before entering the water, the hydraulically operated hinged buoyancy tanks (which are on top of the vehicle when travelling) are swung through 180 degrees into position. The decking is positioned in a few minutes by a light alloy crane which when travelling is on the centreline of the vehicle. When assembled the roadway is 7.62m (25ft) long and 5.48m (18ft) wide. Once in the water, the units are fastened together to form a Class 50 bridge or ferry. Once in the water the M3 is fully amphibious, with one of the engines driving propellers for sideways movement and the other engine driving a steering propeller. One of the two side propellers can also be used for steering. When the M3 is swimming, the wheels are raised to reduce drag. On land all-wheel steering is possible, and there are flotation bags inside the wheel arches for extra flotation. The M2 and M3 systems were specifically developed for operations with the British Army of the Rhine for the crossing of the many waterways in central Europe.

SPECIFICATIONS

Type:	amphibious bridge
Manufacturer:	EKG
Powerplant:	2 x Deutz Model F8 diesels
Horsepower:	178
Transmission:	unknown
Length:	12.73m (41.76ft)
Width:	3.35m (10.99ft)
Height:	3.93m (12.89ft)
Weight:	25,300kg (55,660lb)
Ground clearance:	0.7m (2.29ft)
Armament:	none
Crew:	4
Top speed:	76km/h (47.5mph)
Range:	725km (453 miles)
Fording:	amphibious
Gradient:	60 percent
Configuration:	4 x 4

M60

The chassis of the M60 armoured vehicle launched bridge (AVLB) is almost identical to that of the M60 main battle tank, though the turret has been removed and the driver sits farther back. The vehicle has torsion bar-type suspension which is made up of six road wheels with the idler at the rear, with three track return rollers. The second and sixth road wheel stations have hydraulic shock absorbers. The bridge itself weighs 13,380kg (29,436lb) is made of aluminium. On the vehicle it is carried folded and launched over the front hydraulically. When the vehicle has reached the space to be bridged, the bridge is raised hydraulically into the vertical, unfolded and then lowered into place; the launcher is then detached. In general the procedure takes three minutes, with recovery time being between 10 and 60 minutes depending on terrain conditions. The bridge itself has a length of 19.2m (63ft) and can span a gap up to 18.28m (60ft). In the M60 chassis the engine and transmission are at the rear, and the two-man crew consists of a driver and commander. The earlier M48 AVLB had two Browning 12.7mm machine guns, but the M60 variant has no armament. The M60 bridge layer is now being replaced by more modern and capable systems, such as the Wolverine (see page 16).

SPECIFICATIONS

Type:	mechanized bridge
Manufacturer:	General Dynamics
Powerplant:	Continental AVDS-1790-2A
Horsepower:	750
Transmission:	2 + 1
Length:	11.28m (37ft)
Width:	4m (13.12ft)
Height:	3.9m (12.79ft)
Weight:	55,205kg (121,451lb)
Ground clearance:	0.36m(1.18ft)
Armament:	none
Crew:	2
Top speed:	48.28km/h (30.17mph)
Range:	500km (312 miles)
Fording:	1.21m (3.96ft)
Gradient:	30 percent
Configuration:	tracked

WOLVERINE

The Wolverine is an armoured vehicle designed to carry, emplace and retrieve an assault bridge capable of supporting loads such as the M1A2 main battle tank. The Wolverine is a combat support system which integrates advanced bridging, hydraulic and electronic control capabilities into a single survivable system. Wolverine fills the need for a combat gap crossing capability with the same mobility, survivability and transportability as the M1 Abrams tank. Wolverine will be a one-for-one replacement for the Armoured Vehicle Launched Bridge (AVLB) in select heavy divisional engineer battalions, armoured cavalry regiments and heavy separate brigades. Wolverine consists of an M1 Abrams tank chassis modified to transport, launch and retrieve a Military Load Class (MLC) 70 bridge across gaps up to 24m (78.74ft) wide. It is airportable in the C-5A aircraft and is comparable in mobility and survivability to the Abrams tank. A crew of two will operate the system. The bridge, made of four interchangeable sections, is 26m (85.3ft) long, 4m (13.12ft) wide and weighs 10,886 kg (23,949lb). The system launches through automatic suspension and has redundant launch capability using the vehicle powerpack or slaved from another Wolverine. In an emergency the launch sequence can be accomplished by one man.

SPECIFICATIONS

Type:	*bridging equipment*
Manufacturer:	*General Dynamics*
Powerplant:	*AGT-1500 Turbine*
Horsepower:	*1500*
Transmission:	*4 + 2*
Length:	*13.4m (43.96ft)*
Width:	*3.48m (11.41ft)*
Height:	*3.96m (12.99ft)*
Weight:	*69,800kg (153,560lb)*
Ground clearance:	*0.48m (1.58ft)*
Armament:	*none*
Crew:	*2*
Top speed:	*72km/h (45mph)*
Range:	*416km (260 miles)*
Fording:	*1.21m (4ft)*
Gradient:	*60 percent*
Configuration:	*tracked*

AAVC7A1

The AAVP7A1 is an armoured assault fully tracked amphibious landing vehicle. The vehicle carries troops in water operations from ship to shore, through rough water and surf zones. It also carries troops to inland objectives after ashore. The primary responsibility of the vehicles during an amphibious operation is to spearhead a beach assault. They disembark from ship and come ashore, carrying infantry and supplies to the area to provide a forced entry into the amphibious assault area for the surface assault element. Once the armoured assault vehicles (AAVs) have landed, they can take on several different tasks: manning check points, Military Operations in Urban Terrain missions, escorting food convoys or mechanized patrol. The AAVC7A1 gives a commander a mobile task force communication centre in water operations from ship to shore and to inland objectives after ashore. The system consists of five radio operator stations: three staff stations, and two master stations. The command communications system contains equipment to provided external secure radio transmission between each AAVC7A1 vehicle and other vehicles and radios. Internal communication between each crew station is provided. The first prototype was built in 1979 and the vehicle entered service in 1983.

SPECIFICATIONS

Type:	amphibious command vehicle
Manufacturer:	FMC Corporation
Powerplant:	Cummins Model VT400
Horsepower:	400
Transmission:	6
Length:	7.94m (26.04ft)
Width:	3.27m (10.72ft)
Height:	3.26m (10.69ft)
Weight:	23,072kg (50,758lb)
Ground clearance:	0.4m (1.31ft)
Armament:	1 x 7.62mm
Crew:	3
Top speed:	72km/h (45mph) (land)
Range:	480km (300 miles)
Fording:	amphibious
Gradient:	60 percent
Configuration:	tracked

FOX

The Fox is a rolling laboratory that takes air, water, and ground samples and immediately analyzes them for signs of weapons of mass destruction. The Fox M93A1 Nuclear, Biological and Chemical Reconnaissance System (NBCRS) is intended to improve the survivability and mobility of US Army ground forces by providing increased situational awareness and information superiority to headquarters and combat manoeuvre elements. NBC defence encompasses three major functions: contamination avoidance, protection and decontamination. Contamination avoidance is the concept of avoiding contamination whenever possible and is the focal point of NBC defence doctrine. With the ability to provide rapid, accurate chemical and radiological contamination information to these elements, the NBCRS vehicle forms a key portion of the full-dimensional protection concept. The onboard M21 Remote Sensing Chemical Agent Alarm allows the crew to detect chemical agent clouds as far as 5m (3.12 miles) away. The crew can perform chemical and radiological reconnaissance operations while operating in a shirt-sleeve environment inside the NBCRS vehicle, even while the vehicle is operating in a contaminated area. The Fox saw valuable service with Coalition forces during the 1991 Gulf War.

SPECIFICATIONS

Type:	mobile laboratory
Manufacturer:	General Dynamics
Powerplant:	Mercedes-Benz Model OM
Horsepower:	320
Transmission:	7 + 1
Length:	6.3m (20.66ft)
Width:	2.98m (9.77ft)
Height:	2.3m (7.54ft)
Weight:	17,000kg (37,400lb)
Ground clearance:	0.5m (1.64m)
Armament:	none
Crew:	3
Top speed:	105km/h (65.62mph)
Range:	800km (500 miles)
Fording:	amphibious
Gradient:	70 percent
Configuration:	6 x 6

LAV-C2

The Light Armoured Vehicle-Command and Control (LAV-C2) is an all-terrain, all-weather vehicle with night capabilities. It allows a commander the capability to command, control and communicate (C3) the activities of his forces under full armoured protection. This mobile command station provides field commanders with all necessary resources to control and coordinate light armoured units in all assigned roles. It is air transportable via C-130, C-141, C-5 and CH-53 E aircraft. When combat loaded there are 200 ready rounds and 800 stowed rounds of 7.62mm ammunition. The vehicle can be made fully amphibious within three minutes. Another variant of the LAV is the LAV-C2 Fire Direction Centre (FDC), whose mission is to control and assign fire missions, choose the number and the type of rounds to fire, and provide firing data to eight mortars under platoon operations or four under split section operations. It maintains continuous communications via digital or voice with all platoon elements within its area of responsibility, forward observers, fire support elements and higher headquarters. The FDC performs fire planning and target prioritizing and coordinates with other fire support assets, combat support and combat service support, as needed.

SPECIFICATIONS

Type:	command and control
Manufacturer:	General Motors
Powerplant:	Detroit Diesel 6V53T
Horsepower:	350
Transmission:	5 + 1
Length:	6.42m (21.08ft)
Width:	2.48m (8.16ft)
Height:	2.79m (9.16ft)
Weight:	12,818kg (28,2001b)
Ground clearance:	0.57m (1.87ft)
Armament:	1 x 7.62mm
Crew:	5
Top speed:	100km/h (62mph)
Range:	656km (410 miles)
Fording:	amphibious (with preparation)
Gradient:	60 percent
Configuration:	8 x 8

MEWSS

The Mobile Electronic Warfare Support System (MEWSS) is the US Marine Corps' ground component of the Intelligence and Electronic Warfare Common Sensor (IEWCS) system. It uses the same subsystems as the US Army's Ground Based Common Sensor-Light and Heavy (GBCS-L &GBCS-H), and the Advanced Quickfix (AQF). The MEWSS uses the Light Armored Vehicle (LAV) as its platform. Its mission is as follows: two-way communications, data collection, locating and positioning of enemy forces, jamming and intercepting enemy communications, and the mobile support of friendly units The MEWSS is capable of intercept and location. It is also capable of conducting surgical electronic attacks against designated targets and is is operated in the forward area of operations. The most notable example of IEWCS technology transfer is to the US Marine Corps in an electronics suite upgrade to the Mobile Electronic Warfare Support System (MEWSS), known as the MEWSS Product Improvement Program (MEWSS-PIP). This upgrade utilizes all three IEWCS subsystems configured in a standard Light Armored Vehicle, to become in essence a fourth IEWCS platform configuration. The vehicle can be made fully amphibious, and has a swim speed of 9.6km/h (6mph).

SPECIFICATIONS

Type:	electronic warfare
Manufacturer:	General Motors
Powerplant:	Detroit Diesel 6V53T
Horsepower:	350hp
Transmission:	5 + 1
Length:	6.57m (21.58ft)
Width:	2.49m (8.2ft)
Height:	2.64m (8.66ft)
Weight:	12,818kg (28,200lb)
Ground clearance:	0.5m (1.64ft)
Armament:	1 x 7.62mm
Crew:	5
Top speed:	100km/h (62mph)
Range:	410km (250 miles)
Fording:	amphibious (with preparation)
Gradient:	60 percent
Configuration:	8 x 8

PIRANHA ACV

The Mowag Piranha III family of vehicles offers the features and performances required of a modern, multi-role vehicle, which is well suited to practically any battlefield or peace-keeping/peace-enforcing role anywhere in the world, either as an armoured personnel carrier or an ideal platform for a complete range of weapons systems from small-calibre turrets up to the high firepower of a 105mm gun. The Armoured Command Vehicle (ACV) is in Swedish Navy service, being deployed to the coastal artillery brigades. It is a highly mobile, well protected command, control, communications and information platform whose crew members are protected from light machine-gun rounds and artillery shell splinters by hardened steel plate armour. The crew compartment is fully air conditioned, while the vehicle has been designed to operate in a nuclear, biological and chemical (NBC) environment. The vehicle is highly mobile: a hydropneumatic system with a MOWAG-designed height adjustment system at all wheel stations in combination with the new wheels system with CTIS and ABS and the choice of tyre sizes to suit any type of terrain, as well as high power-to-weight ratio power packs, have resulted in a class of wheeled vehicles with a mobility comparable to tracked vehicles, whilst still retaining air transportability.

SPECIFICATIONS

Type:	command and control
Manufacturer:	Mowag
Powerplant:	Scania DSJ9-48A
Horsepower:	387
Transmission:	7 + 1
Length:	7.91m (25.95ft)
Width:	2.6m (8.53ft)
Height:	2.91m (9.54ft)
Weight:	20,000kg (44,000lb)
Ground clearance:	0.45m (1.47ft)
Armament:	1 x 7.62mm
Crew:	up to 8
Top speed:	100km/h (62.5mph)
Range:	500km (312 miles)
Fording:	1.5m (4.92ft)
Gradient:	60 percent
Configuration:	10 x 10

PIRANHA ASV

The Piranha armoured sensor vehicle (ASV) is in service with the Swedish Navy. It is a highly mobile sensor vehicle for the direction of artillery fire and the detection of both land and air targets. The spacious command room in the rear of the vehicle houses four consoles. The vehicle can be deployed very quickly and can operate in hostile environments. One reason for this is the Piranha'a excellent payload-versus-combat weight qualities. The new Piranha III design provides the customer with flexibility in the choice of protection levels and equipment/weapons integration and personnel transport. Through the modular concept, the question is how much payload/volume is required and not the number of axles/wheels, because the front section of the vehicle, including the two front steered axles, is identical on the 6 x 6, 8 x 8 and 10 x 10 versions of the Piranha III vehicles. The use of the Piranha family vehicles by peace-keeping forces has proven the inherent protection of the vehicle design, especially against mines. The knowledge gained through the experiences of the peace-keeping missions, for example in former Yugoslavia and Somalia, has been implemented in the variable protection concept, which allows ballistic protection to be tailored to meet the expected threat in each mission scenario.

SPECIFICATIONS

Type:	fire direction vehicle
Manufacturer:	Mowag
Powerplant:	Scania DSJ9-48A
Horsepower:	400hp
Transmission:	7 + 1
Length:	9.6m (31.49ft)
Width:	2.6m (8.33ft)
Height:	3.82m (12.53ft)
Weight:	23,000kg (50,600lb)
Ground clearance:	0.45m (1.47ft)
Armament:	1 x 7.62mm
Crew:	6
Top speed:	100km/h (62mph)
Range:	450km (281 miles)
Fording:	1.5m (4.92ft)
Gradient:	60 percent
Configuration:	10 x 10

XA-202

This is the XA-202 Command Version of the XA-200 series. It features a hydraulic mast and communications gear. The vehicle is well armoured and heavily modified, the heavy machine-gun mount has been moved from the crew compartment hatch to the vehicle commander's hatch. The telescopic mast is powered by the main engine hydraulic pump and has hydraulic support legs for the vehicle and an automatic guy rope system of 5.2m (17.06ft) radius with hydraulic tightening system. The mast takes two people about 10 minutes to deploy. The hull is divided into four sections: operator room, driver/commander compartment, engine room and auxiliary power unit (APU) room. The 10 kW diesel APU is installed for the operator room equipment. Add-on armour provides protection from up to 12.7mm armour-piercing shells. There are four fitting points for VHF antennas. The add-on armour plates can be added by the crew thanks to their relatively small size and with maximum armour the amphibious capabilities are only partially lost. The vehicle can still, however, drive through 1.5m (4.92ft) of water. If a client demands both heavy armour and amphibious capability, the vehicle can be modified to solve this problem without compromising the armour protection or the amphibious characteristics.

SPECIFICATIONS

Type:	command vehicle
Manufacturer:	Patria
Powerplant:	Valmet 612 turbocharged diesel
Horsepower:	270
Transmission:	6 + 1
Length:	7.41m (24.31ft)
Width:	2.92m (9.58ft)
Height:	2.92m (9.58ft)
Weight:	23,000kg (50,600lb)
Ground clearance:	0.45m (1.47ft)
Armament:	1 x 12.7mm machine gun
Crew:	2 + 4
Top speed:	90km/h (56.25mph)
Range:	600km (375 miles)
Fording:	1.2m (3.93ft)
Gradient:	60 percent
Configuration:	6 x 6

ATLAS

The ATLAS is the next generation military, variable reach, rough terrain forklift vehicle selected by the Department of the Army. It is capable of lifting 4545kg (10,000lb). The front end quick attach feature can accommodate dual carriages of 2727kg (6000lb) and 4545kg (10,000lb) each. The intended use of the ATLAS includes selecting stock from storage; stuffing and unstuffing containers; and unloading, transporting, and loading boxes. It is capable of mobility in rough terrain and is transportable in C-130 aircraft. The ATLAS System Description is a four-wheel drive, pneumatic tired, diesel engine-driven, variable reach, boom type forklift truck with a maximum speed of 23mph. The rated capacity of the ATLAS is 2727kg (6000lb) at 0.6m (2ft) load centre (with a 2727kg [6000lb] capacity carriage mounted) and 10000lb at 1.21m (4ft) load centre (with the 4545kg [10,000lb] capacity carriage mounted). TRAK International manufactured the 6000M variable reach forklifts between 1989 and 1993 and delivered over 2200 vehicles to the US armed forces. These logistic support vehicles performed exceedingly well during Operation Desert Storm in 1991 and in Bosnia handling missiles, ammunition, and supplies in the toughest types of terrain in direct support of deployed military forces.

SPECIFICATIONS

Type:	*forklift*
Manufacturer:	*TRAK*
Powerplant:	*Cummins 4BT3 diesel*
Horsepower:	*116*
Transmission:	*4 + 3*
Length:	*4.3m (14.1ft)*
Width:	*2.5m (8.2ft)*
Height:	*3m (9.84ft)*
Weight:	*11,951kg (26,323lb)*
Ground clearance:	*0.44m (1.44ft)*
Armament:	*none*
Crew:	*1*
Top speed:	*32km/h (20mph)*
Range:	*400km (250 miles)*
Fording:	*unknown*
Gradient:	*60 percent*
Configuration:	*4 x 4*

BM 440

The BM 440 has been specifically designed to handle North Atlantic Treaty Organization (NATO) pallets. IN addition, other design features have been included for military use. With the break up of the Warsaw Pact and the USSR, the emphasis for Western European and American forces has switched from a confrontation in central Europe to peace-keeping in Europe and military operations outside the European theatre. Armed forces therefore need to be able to move quickly at relatively short notice, and their logistical backup has to be similarly mobile. Therefore, the BM 440 has a low-profile cab for air portability. It also has a high road speed to enable it to keep up with convoys, and can also be towed at convoy speeds. The operator's cab is mounted at the front to provide good visibility with minimum engine noise and vibration. It has a forward reach capability to allow loading and unloading from one side of a cargo truck or rail wagon. Power-operated steering reduces driver discomfort, and the forklift can be fitted with a range of attachments, including buckets and sweepers to increase its versatility. The models shown above are in service with the British Army, and are painted white because they part of a United Nations commitment.

SPECIFICATIONS

Type:	forklift
Manufacturer:	Volvo
Powerplant:	TAD420 diesel
Horsepower:	140
Transmission:	4 + 3
Length:	5.62m (18.43ft)
Width:	2.54 (8.33ft)
Height:	2.67m (8.75ft)
Weight:	7000kg (15,400lb)
Ground clearance:	0.4m (1.31ft)
Armament:	none
Crew:	1
Top speed:	60km/h (37.5mph)
Range:	500km (312 miles)
Fording:	0.75m (2.46ft)
Gradient:	60 percent
Configuration:	4 x 4

M320.42 WM

Iveco of Italy produces a range of light, medium and heavy military trucks unrivalled by any other manufacturer in the world. Iveco trucks are in active service throughout the world supported by a comprehensive international dealer organization. Their range is very comprehensive: at the light end of the weight range is a 4 x 4 with a payload of 1500kg (3300lb) based on the class-leading Turbo Daily chassis. This highly flexible vehicle can be adapted for use in a wide variety of rolls, including troop transporter, command post, light gun tractor and ambulance. Moving to higher-capacity vehicles, a recent addition to the range is the outstanding Multipurpose Military Vehicle – (MMV). This is a high-mobility 4 x 4 offroad truck with a payload capability of up to 6400kg. It is C-130 Hercules transportable and the cab area is easily armoured with the addition of appliqué panels. Available in three engine sizes, three wheel base lengths and with manual or automatic transmissions, the MMV can be tailored to meet a wide variety of military uses. The M320 mobile crane is just one of Iveco's products. With outriggers the crane can lift up to 30,000kg (66,000lb), while without outriggers the load that can be lifted can be up to 8500kg (18,700lb). This means it can lift both trucks and light armoured fighting vehicles.

SPECIFICATIONS

Type:	mobile crane
Manufacturer:	Iveco
Powerplant:	Iveco CURSOR 10 diesel
Horsepower:	420
Transmission:	6 + 6
Length:	10m (32.8ft)
Width:	2.13m (7ft)
Height:	3.03m (9.94ft)
Weight:	12,200kg (26,840lb)
Ground clearance:	0.5m (1.64ft)
Armament:	none
Crew:	1
Top speed:	90km/h (56.25mph)
Range:	500km (312 miles)
Fording:	1m (3.28ft)
Gradient:	60 percent
Configuration:	8 x 8

RTCC

The Grove Manufacturing Corporation produces a number of mobile hydraulic cranes for the military and civilian markets. The Rough Terrain Container Crane (RTCC) has a galvanized steel cab which has an opening skylight with electric wiper, deluxe seat with arm rest-integrated crane controls, hydraulic oil heater plus drive and steering controls. The RTCC is built for heavy work. For example, it has four hydraulically telescoping beams with "inverted" jacks and outrigger pads. Each one has independent horizontal and vertical movement control from the crane operator's cab. The vehicle has a standard Graphic Display load moment and anti-block system with audio-visual warning and control lever lock-out. These systems provide electronic display of boom angle, length, radius, tip height, relative load moment, maximum permissible load, and load indication. The main and auxiliary hoists each have two vane motors, planetary gear and dual speed with automatic spring-applied multi-disc brakes. The company produces five types of hydraulic cranes for the military market: truck-mounted cranes, rough terrain cranes, all-purpose warehouse cranes, all terrain cranes and hydraulic lattice boom cranes. There are nearly 300 RTCCs currently in US Army service.

SPECIFICATIONS

Type:	*rough terrain crane*
Manufacturer:	*Grove Manufacturing Corporation*
Powerplant:	*Cummins 6CTA diesel*
Horsepower:	*250*
Transmission:	*6 + 6*
Length:	*14.34m (47.04ft)*
Width:	*3.34m (10.95ft)*
Height:	*3.97m (13.02ft)*
Weight:	*49,500kg (108,900)*
Ground clearance:	*0.53m (1.73ft)*
Armament:	*none*
Crew:	*1*
Top speed:	*40km/h (25mph)*
Range:	*400km (250 miles)*
Fording:	*unknown*
Gradient:	*76 percent*
Configuration:	*8 x 8*

RTCH

The Army Standard 50K Rough Terrain Container Handler (RTCH) is a modified commercial truck which is essentially a Caterpillar model 988B wheel loader with a CAT model AH60 forklift mast. It is used in conjunction with 6.09m (20ft), 10.66m (35ft) or 12.19m (40ft) top handler attachments for lifting containers weighing up to 25,000kg (55,000lb). In its standard configuration, the RTCH can stack containers two high. It is designed to function over rough terrain and through salt water up to 1.52m (5ft). Its primary use is in holding and marshalling areas by selected supply, ammunition and transportation units. There are two known non-standard variants of the RTCH. The first results from the installation of a fork kit that was issued only to Fort Eustis concurrent with the initial fielding of the RTCH. So equipped, the RTCH can function as a rough terrain forklift. This fork kit is not currently available in the US Army supply system. The second RTCH variant comes from installing a low-mount fork assembly that allows the RTCH to lift half-height – 1.29m (4.25ft) – containers. Sixty-two kits were fielded between April and September 1992. Fort Eustis has about half of all those produced. This half height kit is not available through the US Army supply system.

SPECIFICATIONS

Type:	forklift
Manufacturer:	Caterpillar
Powerplant:	Caterpillar 3408
Horsepower:	393
Transmission:	powershift
Length:	10.73m (35.2ft)
Width:	3.5m (11.48ft)
Height:	4.11m (13.48ft)
Weight:	5000kg (11,000lb)
Ground clearance:	0.4m (1.31ft)
Armament:	none
Crew:	1
Top speed:	40km/h (25mph)
Range:	unknown
Fording:	1.52m (4.98ft)
Gradient:	30 percent
Configuration:	4 x 4

RV730

This vehicle is designed for recovery operations of tracked vehicles. It is based on a 6 x 6 chassis and is built for heavy recovery operations, winching, towing and hoisting. The main recovery winch has a capacity of 20,000kg (44,000lb) single pull and is mounted in the slewing frame of the crane. The mounting of the winch in the slewing crane base means that the object is always being pulled in a direct line towards the recovery vehicle, thus facilitating the lifting of heavy loads. The crane itself is hydraulically operated between horizontal and 70 degrees, and the arm has a hydraulic telescopic extension that works with a full load. The crane can be operated from the seat of the crane base or from a remote-control unit. At the rear of the vehicle is a lifting/towing boom that is hydraulically operated; it has a maximum lifting capacity of 6000kg (13,200lb). Mounted behind the cab are locked cabinets that accommodate tools and accessories necessary for the lifting mission. The outriggers are used as anchoring spades and have been designed so that each one can carry the pulling force of 40,000kg (88,000lb). However, this is possible only when loads are being pulled from the rear. Sideways, the pulling force is limited to 15,000kg (33,000lb).

SPECIFICATIONS

Type:	recovery vehicle
Manufacturer:	Hägglunds Moelv
Powerplant:	DS11 diesel
Horsepower:	305
Transmission:	9 + 1
Length:	8.8m (28.87ft)
Width:	2.5m (8.2ft)
Height:	3.25m (10.66ft)
Weight:	21,000kg (46,200lb)
Ground clearance:	0.45m (1.47ft)
Armament:	none
Crew:	1
Top speed:	100km/h (62.5mph)
Range:	500km (312 miles)
Fording:	1.1m (3.6ft)
Gradient:	30 percent
Configuration:	6 x 6

AEV

The German Armoured Engineer Vehicle (AEV) is based on the Leopard 1 main battle tank chassis. It has been modified by replacing the turret with a new welded top structure. In addition, the AEV is equipped with a dozer blade, excavator and two winches. The dozer blade has two rippers for tearing up roads and other hard surfaces, and the dozer itself can be tilted, elevated and skewed thanks to a unique hydraulic design. The main use of the blade is for digging, though the blade can also be used as a soil anchor when operating the winches or the excavator. The AEV has a hinged excavator arm mounted on a turntable at the centre front of the vehicle. The excavator has a digging sector of around 175 percent at the front of the vehicle with operation similar to commercial excavators. There is also a grabbing claw for lifting timber logs which is fitted to the underside of the excavator arm. The two hydraulic capstan winches are designed for the recovery of other vehicles plus self-recovery. They provide great flexibility and have a pulling power of up to 60,000kg (132,000lb). The two-man crew are under armour protection in the vehicle at all times, allowing for excavating to be carried out under enemy fire. The AEV is a valuable asset in the German Army arsenal.

SPECIFICATIONS

Type:	armoured engineer vehicle
Manufacturer:	Hägglunds Moelv
Powerplant:	MTU MB 838 Ca M500
Horsepower:	830
Transmission:	4 + 2
Length:	10m (32.8ft)
Width:	3.6m (11.81ft)
Height:	3m (9.84ft)
Weight:	46,000kg (101,200lb)
Ground clearance:	0.44m (1.44ft)
Armament:	none
Crew:	2
Top speed:	62km/h (38.75mph)
Range:	650km (406 miles)
Fording:	4m (13.12ft)
Gradient:	50 percent
Configuration:	tracked

AVRE

This British Assault Vehicle Royal Engineers (AVRE) consists of a Chieftain main battle tank with the turret and all armament removed and a metal plate fitted that covers the turret ring. The driver's position remains unaltered with a hatch, but the AVRE commander's position has been fitted with a hatch. Over the entire length of the vehicle are two rails, on which up to three maxi-pipe fascines or up to five rolls of Class 60 trackway can be carried. They are unloaded by raising the rails at the rear. At the front of the vehicle is a dozer blade or mine plough and at the rear is a winch. In the centre of the AVRE is a crane with a telescopic jib. This vehicle, of which 50 are in operation with the British Army, is a replacement for the Centurion AVRE that had been in service since the 1960s. The AVRE can also tow the Giant Viper mine-clearing equipment, which consists of a hose filled with plastic explosives that is packed coiled in box mounted on a two-wheel trailer. The hose is fired across a minefield by a cluster of eight rocket motors, and then detonates once it has landed. The crew of the AVRE consists of three men, and no armament is carried other than personal small arms. A dozer blade can also be fitted to the vehicle for the clearing of mines.

SPECIFICATIONS

Type:	*armoured engineer vehicle*
Manufacturer:	*Royal Ordnance*
Powerplant:	*Roll-Royce CV12*
Horsepower:	*730*
Transmission:	*5 + 2*
Length:	*10m (32.8ft)*
Width:	*3.92m(12.86ft)*
Height:	*3m (9.84ft)*
Weight:	*49,000kg (107,800lb)*
Ground clearance:	*0.46m (1.5ft)*
Armament:	*none*
Crew:	*3*
Top speed:	*34km/h (21.25mph)*
Range:	*176km (110 miles)*
Fording:	*1.45m (4.75ft)*
Gradient:	*60 percent*
Configuration:	*tracked*

BADGER

The Badger armoured engineer vehicle is based on the Leopard 1 main battle tank, and was developed to meet the special needs of the German Army and combines well-proven components with advanced technology. Its features include extendible dozer blade, scarifiers and cutting and welding equipment, powerful telescopic excavator and an electrically controlled hydraulic system. Like other members of the Leopard family, the Badger has a deep fording capacity of 4m (13.12ft), and even when operating under water many operational functions are still possible. For example, the vehicle can be underwater in a river while its excavator can be working on one of the river banks. Reflecting the changing role of many of Western Europe's armed forces, Badger has proved a reliable vehicle for defence and peace-keeping missions, as well as for disaster relief operations. They have been successfully deployed in various UN and peace-keeping operations. Its main missions are as follows: preparing river crossings, preparing and removing obstacles and blockades on the battlefield, recovery assistance for deep-fording and underwater main battle tanks, loading loose materials and debris on to trucks, lifting loads during pioneer missions, and the general recovery of vehicles and equipment both on and off the battlefield.

SPECIFICATIONS

Type:	armoured engineer vehicle
Manufacturer:	Rheinmetall
Powerplant:	MTU MB 838 Ca M500
Horsepower:	830
Transmission:	4 + 2
Length:	8.37m (27.46ft)
Width:	3.25m (10.66ft)
Height:	2.57m (8.43ft)
Weight:	43,000kg (94,600lb)
Ground clearance:	0.44m (1.44ft)
Armament:	none
Crew:	3
Top speed:	62km/h (38.75mph)
Range:	650km (406 miles)
Fording:	4m (13.12ft)
Gradient:	50 percent
Configuration:	tracked

BUFFALO

The Buffalo armoured recovery vehicle (ARV) was specifically designed to support the Leopard 2 main battle tank in both the German and Dutch armies and it was developed, produced and delivered to them by Rheinmetall Landsysteme as general contractor. By using the Leopard 2 chassis and proven and modified Leopard 2 assemblies, combined with a powerful recovery system, Rheinmetall Landsysteme has created a recovery vehicle which is superior in its class and meets all mission-related requirements. The Buffalo is equipped with a 35,000kg (77,000lb) capstan winch, a 30,000kg (66,000lb) crane system, an integrated test system and a support and dozer system. Future Buffalos will have a new navigation and control system, a performance-improved auxiliary winch and a liner interior protection system, as well as an advanced optical system for reverse cruise. Upon request, a special launch system for various ammunition, including high-explosive ammunition, can be installed. The missions of the vehicle include the recovery of tracked vehicles out of trenches and rivers, towing tracked vehicles, the recovery of main battles tanks, plus general dozing and obstacles removal duties. Spain and Sweden have placed orders for this Leopard 2-based ARV.

SPECIFICATIONS

Type:	armoured recovery vehicle
Manufacturer:	Rheinmetall
Powerplant:	MTU MB 873 Ka-501
Horsepower:	850hp
Transmission:	4 + 2
Length:	9.07m (29.75ft)
Width:	3.54m (11.61ft)
Height:	2.99m (9.8ft)
Weight:	54,300kg (119,460lb)
Ground clearance:	0.51m (1.67ft)
Armament:	none
Crew:	3
Top speed:	68km/h (42.5mph)
Range:	650km (406 miles)
Fording:	4m (13.12ft)
Gradient:	60 percent
Configuration:	tracked

CEBARV

C EBARV, the Centurion Beach Armoured Recovery
Vehicle, is the only recovery vehicle in service in the
United Kingdom in the amphibious role. Developed
from the Centurion main battle tank with a prefabricated
turret to enable it to ford up to depths of 2.9m (9.51ft).
The main tasks of the CEBARV are to recover drowned or
broken vehicles; to push off beached landing craft using its
built-in special nose block; and to provide a breakwater
for small craft and men operating in the water. The CEBARV
will be replaced by the Future Beach Recovery Vehicle
(FBRV) for the UK's Royal Marines, and it has now been
delivered to the UK by prime contractor Hägglunds
Moelv of Norway. The FBRV is based on a German
Krauss-Maffei Wegmann Leopard 1 main battle tank chassis
especially modified for the new mission. It will replace the
current Centurion Beach Armoured Recovery Vehicle ,
which was based on a Centurion Mk 3 main battle tank
chassis. The FBRV will be used for a wide range of roles
including unbeaching, unbroaching and anchoring of
landing craft as well as the recovery of drowned vehicles.
In addition, it will provide a lee for recovery and diving
operations. The beach recovery vehicle is certainly among
the most unusual elements in the British arsenal.

SPECIFICATIONS

Type:	beach recovery vehicle
Manufacturer:	Vickers Defence
Powerplant:	Meteor Mk 6
Horsepower:	650
Transmission:	5 + 2
Length:	8.07m (26.47ft)
Width:	3.4m (11.15ft)
Height:	3.45m (11.31ft)
Weight:	40,000kg (88,000lb)
Ground clearance:	0.45m (1.47ft)
Armament:	none
Crew:	4
Top speed:	33.7km/h (21mph)
Range:	400km (250 miles)
Fording:	2.9m (9.51ft)
Gradient:	60 percent
Configuration:	tracked

CET

The Combat Engineer Tractor (CET) provides support for the British Army battle group by carrying out excavating earth, preparation of river banks, road repair, recovering damaged vehicles and preparing or clearing obstacles. The hull is made of aluminium, and inside the hull the driver sits at the front and operates the winch, with the bucket operator to his rear. Both crew members can reverse their seats to carry out each other's duties if need be. The crew compartment itself is provided with two hatch covers and 10 vision blocks, and is fully air conditioned. The engine and transmission are mounted at the right side of the hull with the final drives being mounted at the front of the hull. The CET has torsion bar-type suspension with five road wheels (the fifth one acts as the idler). The tracks are made of cast steel with rubber bushes and rubber pads are supplied to reduce wear when operating on roads. With preparation the CET is fully amphibious, with steering in the water carried out by deflecting the thrust from water jets mounted on either side of the hull. The two-speed winch has a maximum pull of 8000kg (17,600lb) and is provided with 113m (37ft) of cable. The vehicle also has a rocket-launched ground anchor (shown being fired in the above photograph).

SPECIFICATIONS

Type:	armoured engineer vehicle
Manufacturer:	Royal Ordnance
Powerplant:	Rolls-Royce C6TFR diesel
Horsepower:	320
Transmission:	4 + 4
Length:	7.3m (23.95ft)
Width:	2.76m (9.05ft)
Height:	3.41m (11.18ft)
Weight:	17,700kg (38,940lb)
Ground clearance:	0.45m (1.47ft)
Armament:	1 x 7.62mm
Crew:	2
Top speed:	56km/h (35mph)
Range:	320km (200 miles)
Fording:	1.63m (5.34ft)
Gradient:	60 percent
Configuration:	tracked

CRRAV

CRRAV – Challenger Repair and Recovery Armoured Vehicle – is the most powerful armoured recovery vehicle available today. Its winch capacity enables it to undertake over 80 percent of recovery tasks on a 65,000kg (143,000lb) main battle tank with a single line pull. Its crane has a lift capacity of 6500kg (14,300lb) for automotive assembly exchange and it is fitted with a full electric arc welding facility, air compressor with power tools and track cutter. Its hydraulically operated dozer blade acts as an earth anchor during winching operations, enabling it to exert a maximum line pull of 100,000kg, (220,000lb) as well as making it capable of moving large volumes of soil and digging tank scrapes. The majority of CRRAV's repair and recovery equipment is hydraulically powered. It makes maximum use of major automotive sub-systems and components common to the Challenger 2 main battle tank, which enhances its ability to remain on station with, and give close support to, Challenger 2-equipped battle groups. CRRAV has been developed with reliability and maintainability as major design factors. A comprehensive logistic support package, covering every aspect of training, spares and engineering support, keeps the vehicle at the peak of operational effectiveness.

SPECIFICATIONS

Type:	repair & recovery vehicle
Manufacturer:	Vickers Defence Systems
Powerplant:	Perkins CV 12 diesel
Horsepower:	1200
Transmission:	6 + 2
Length:	9.59m (31.46ft)
Width:	3.62m (11.87ft)
Height:	3m (9.84ft)
Weight:	62,000kg (136,400lb)
Ground clearance:	0.5m (1.64ft)
Armament:	1 x 7.62mm
Crew:	3 + 2
Top speed:	59km/h (36.87mph)
Range:	500km (312 miles)
Fording:	1.07m (3.51ft)
Gradient:	58 percent
Configuration:	tracked

CS-563

The CS-433C and CS-563D Vibratory Rollers are both built by Caterpillar in the United States. The CS-433C Vibratory Roller is a commercial compactor which has been modified and manufactured for distribution to military engineers for their compaction requirements. Caterpillar vehicles are an integral part of US Army engineer operations. The CS-433C is equipped with military modifications such as lifting eyes/tie-downs to permit military transport. It also contains a rifle bracket, and in its military configuration a top coat of CARC paint is applied. The machine is capable of compacting a 0.3m (1ft) lift at the rate of 734 cubic yards per hour to a level of 95 on the Proctor scale. The CS-563C Vibratory Roller (pictured) is currently being manufactured for the military engineers for their compaction missions. It contains all of the attributes explained above for the CS-433C, but, in addition, it is capable of compacting a 0.3m (1ft) lift at the rate of 1907 cubic yards per hour. Both compactors are air deployable and have C-130 Drive-On/Drive-Off capabilities. The CS-433C can also be deployed by Low Velocity Air Drop (LVAD). Both machines come equipped with a smooth drum and a pad foot shell kit or pad foot drum and a levelling blade.

SPECIFICATIONS

Type:	roller
Manufacturer:	Caterpillar
Powerplant:	Caterpillar 3116T diesel
Horsepower:	153
Transmission:	unknown
Length:	4.57m (15ft)
Width:	2.13m (7ft)
Height:	2.74m (9ft)
Weight:	10,875kg (23,925lb)
Ground clearance:	0.48m (1.57ft)
Armament:	none
Crew:	1
Top speed:	6.4km/h (4mph)
Range:	unknown
Fording:	unknown
Gradient:	60 percent
Configuration:	wheels & roller

DEUCE

Caterpillar has designed and manufactured a new high-speed dozer for the US Army, the Deployable Universal Combat Earthmover, or DEUCE. These machines perform typical engineering missions, such as vehicle/crew fighting positions, force protection for command posts, artillery and logistics, and disaster relief such as floods. The DEUCE features Caterpillar's Mobil-Trac System (MTS) rubber-belted undercarriage for onroad and offroad mobility and flotation. The DEUCE is a 35,500lb (16,140kg) earthmover capable of highway speeds of over 48km/h (30mph). The hydro-pneumatic suspension can be engaged for cross-country traverses or locked out to provide a stable dozing platform. Two modes of operation – self-deployable for high-speed travel, and earthmoving for dozing – are designed to provide optimum performance for mission flexibility. The DEUCE can be prepared for air drops by two mechanics in less than 20 minutes, and can be re-assembled in less than 30 minutes. C-130 Drive-on/Drive-off preparation takes less than 10 minutes to collapse the front suspension cylinders to lower overall height. Maintainability is a built-in feature of the DEUCE, and accessibility to filters, batteries and fluid sight gauges is easily accomplished.

SPECIFICATIONS

Type:	earthmover
Manufacturer:	Caterpillar
Powerplant:	Caterpillar Model 3126 diesel
Horsepower:	265
Transmission:	automatic
Length:	6.42m (21.08ft)
Width:	2.94m (9.66ft)
Height:	2.71m (8.91ft)
Weight:	16,136kg (35,000lb)
Ground clearance:	0.3m (1ft)
Armament:	none
Crew:	1
Top speed:	52.8km/h (33mph)
Range:	320km (200 miles)
Fording:	0.91m (3ft)
Gradient:	30 percent
Configuration:	tracked

FODEN RECOVERY VEHICLE

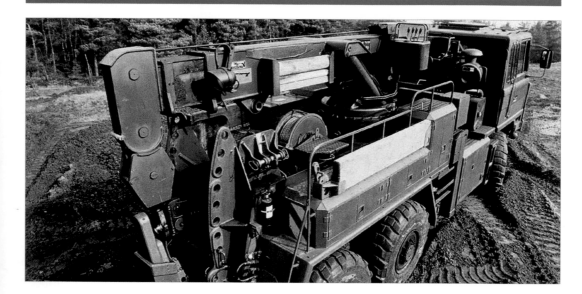

This is a heavy recovery vehicle employed primarily in support of the wheeled logistic vehicle fleet to recover immobilized vehicles as a result of bogging, breakdown or damage. Fitted with an hydraulically operated winch/crane in conjunction with outriggers to lift and recover as required. Slewing cranes, which could be used for various lifting tasks in addition to suspended tows during recovery, were deemed important, thus the Foden vehicle featured a pedestal mounted crane. In addition, instead of having hydraulic rams to raise the main recovery supporting boom, it was lifted by the crane. Once at the required height, either for stowage or with a casualty attached, the boom was locked into position, with pins passing through quadrants on each side of the channel in which the boom moved. This removed the weight from the crane itself which in some cases was then necessarily stowed off the centreline in order to clear the raised boom and casualty. Hydraulic systems were retained to operate the side stabilizers used during crane operations, the rear spade anchors and also a rear axle lockout system. Another feature is a remote-control cable system for operating switches. This allows the recovery mechanic to stand next to the casualty and observe closely while controlling lifts or winching.

SPECIFICATIONS

Type:	recovery vehicle
Manufacturer:	Foden
Powerplant:	Perkins Eagle diesel
Horsepower:	290
Transmission:	9-speed constant mesh
Length:	9.06m (29.72ft)
Width:	2.48m (8.13ft)
Height:	3.35m (10.99ft)
Weight:	25,338kg (55,744lb)
Ground clearance:	0.42m (1.37ft)
Armament:	none
Crew:	1
Top speed:	97km/h (60.62mph)
Range:	500km (312 miles)
Fording:	1.22m (4ft)
Gradient:	33 percent
Configuration:	6 x 6

LAV-R

The Light Armoured Vehicle-Recovery (LAV-R) is an all-terrain, all-weather vehicle with night capabilities. This vehicle is capable of safely uprighting overturned LAVs while minimizing additional damage. It has the tactical mobility to reach and recover/support disabled vehicles. The vehicle is capable of towing a disabled LAV with suspension damage. It is air transportable via C-130, C-141, C-5 and CH-53 E aircraft. The vehicle can be made fully amphibious within three minutes. Though a recovery vehicle, it has the means for self-defence, being equipped with a pintle mount for an M240E 7.62mm machine gun, M257 smoke grenade launchers, 200 rounds of 7.62mm ammunition and a further 800 rounds of 7.62mm ammunition stowed. It has the following hatches: overlapping rear doors, rigger's hatch with left and right covers, commander's hatch, driver's hatch, engine compartment hatch and grills, and front stowage compart-ment hatch. Communications systems include AN/VIC-2C Intercom System, VHF SINCGARS radios, VHF radio AN/PRC-68 (stowed), UHF Position Location Reporting System and antenna. The boom crane has a 256-degree traverse, remote control, overload protection, two outrig-gers and two stabilizers.

SPECIFICATIONS

Type:	recovery/support
Manufacturer:	General Motors
Powerplant:	Detroit Diesel 6V53T diesel
Horsepower:	275
Transmission:	5 + 1
Length:	7.24m (24.16ft)
Width:	2.77m (9.08ft)
Height:	2.72m (8.92ft)
Weight:	12,857kg (28,320lb)
Ground clearance:	0.5m (1.64ft)
Armament:	1 x 7.62mm
Crew:	3
Top speed:	100 km/h (62mph)
Range:	656km (410 miles)
Fording:	amphibious
Gradient:	60 percent
Configuration:	8 x 8

M9 ACE

The M9 Armoured Combat Earthmover (ACE) is a highly mobile, armoured, amphibious combat earthmover capable of supporting forces in both offensive and defensive operations. It performs critical combat engineer tasks such as digging fighting positions for guns, tanks and other battlefield systems to increase their survivability. The ACE breaches berms, prepares anti-tank ditches, prepares combat roads, removes roadblocks and prepares access routes at water obstacles. The engine, drive train and driver's compartment are laid out in the rear of the vehicle, while the front features a bowl, apron and dozer blade. Armour consists of welded aluminum with selected steel and aramid-laminated plates. An armoured cupola containing eight vision blocks covers the driver's compartment. The vehicle hull is a welded and bolted aluminum structure with a two-speed winch, and towing pintle and airbrake connections are provided. It is equipped with a unique suspension system which allows the front of the vehicle to be raised, lowered or tilted to permit dozing, excavating, rough grading and ditching functions. In addition, the M9 has armour protection against small-arms and artillery fragmentation, a smoke screening capability and chemical and biological protection for the operator.

SPECIFICATIONS

Type:	armoured earthmover
Manufacturer:	HARSCO Corporation
Powerplant:	Cummins V903C
Horsepower:	295
Transmission:	6 + 2
Length:	6.24m (20.5ft)
Width:	3.2m (10.49ft)
Height:	2.66m (8.75ft)
Weight:	25,000kg (55,000lb)
Ground clearance:	0.33m (1.1ft)
Armament:	none
Crew:	1
Top speed:	48km/h (30mph)
Range:	368km (230 miles)
Fording:	0.91m (3ft)
Gradient:	60 percent
Configuration:	tracked

M88A1

ased on the suspension and running gear of the M48A2 tank, the M88 can be used for both medium and heavy recovery operations using an "A" frame-type hoisting boom. The superstructure and crew compartment is composed of a single large armour casting and provides protection against most types of machine guns and artillery fragments. First accepted into the US Army's inventory in 1959, over 1000 M88s were produced by Bowen-McLaughin-York of Pennsylvania and powered by a Continental AVSI-1790-6A engine with an Allison XT-1400-2 transmission. The crew comprise commander, driver, mechanic and rigger. Both the driver and mechanic are located at the front of the crew compartment with the driver on the left side. The commander is in the centre under the cupola with the rigger directly behind him. Each crew member has a hatch in the roof of the cab, the commander has his cupola and there is also a door in each side of the superstructure. Armament is a 12.7mm machine gun externally mounted on the vehicle commander's cupola. The US Army and US Marines developed a bulldozer blade which could be retrofitted to an M48A3 tank (then designated M8A3). The M88 is still in service with the US Army and with the Israeli Army.

SPECIFICATIONS

Type:	recovery vehicle
Manufacturer:	BMY Combat Systems Division
Powerplant:	12-cylinder diesel
Horsepower:	750
Transmission:	combined transmission
Length:	8.27m (27.13ft)
Width:	3.43m (11.25ft)
Height:	3.13m (10.26ft)
Weight:	50,803kg (111,766lb)
Ground clearance:	0.43m (1.41ft)
Armament:	1 x 12.7mm
Crew:	4
Top speed:	42km/h (26.25mph)
Range:	300 miles (187 miles)
Fording:	1.4m (4.6ft)
Gradient:	60 percent
Configuration:	tracked

M728

The M728 is a fully tracked armoured vehicle which consists of a basic M60A1 tank with a hydraulically operated debris blade, a 165mm turret mounted demolition gun, a retractable boom and a winch. The demolition gun may be elevated or depressed for use at various ranges and is coaxial mounted with a 7.62mm machine gun. A .50-calibre machine gun is cupola mounted. A mine-clearing rake was specially designed and fabricated to be a "tool" for the M728 in Desert Storm. The M728 was placed in service in 1965 with a total of 291 vehicles. Currently, improvements for the vehicle are being implemented, which will ensure that the M728 remains a valuable asset until replacement vehicles are fielded. During Operation Desert Storm in 1991 it proved unable to manoeuvre with the heavy force due to the inability of the M60 chassis and power train to keep pace with the MIA1 tanks. There were also difficulties associated with maintaining an obsolete, low-density piece of equipment. Such was the case with the mine rake mounted on the M728. Many manoeuvre units simply left the M728 behind rather than slow their advance. Commanders planned for their use as a part of a deliberate breaching operation, but left them behind once they began the pursuit and exploitation phase of the operation.

SPECIFICATIONS

Type:	combat engineer vehicle
Manufacturer:	Detroit Tank Arsenal
Powerplant:	Continental AVDS diesel
Horsepower:	750
Transmission:	2 + 1
Length:	8.97m (29.42ft)
Width:	3.71m (12.17ft)
Height:	3.23m (10.59ft)
Weight:	52,200kg (114,840lb)
Ground clearance:	0.45m (1.47ft)
Armament:	1 x 165mm
Crew:	4
Top speed:	50km/h (31.25mph)
Range:	450km (281 miles)
Fording:	1.2m (3.93ft)
Gradient:	60 percent
Configuration:	tracked

SAMSON

When the CVR(T) series of aluminium armoured light vehicles was designed, a full range of variants was considered including an armoured recovery vehicle. The basic hull of the Spartan was adapted to contain a winch which was operated to the rear of the vehicle. A hinged spade anchor was designed in two halves to preserve access to the rear door. To winch any heavy vehicles or lighter ones from difficult slopes, it is necessary to lay out several pulleys to get the maximum effect from a fairly low-capacity winch. The CVR(T) series of vehicles came into use in the early 1970s and most types are still current. Armoured regiments, infantry battalions and similarly sized units with large amounts of equipment have their own Royal Engineers Light Aid Detachment (LAD), commanded by a captain. These units deploy with their parent unit and are equipped with vehicles such as the Samson. An LAD can vary in size from 25 to 90 personnel, depending on the equipment supported. As the name suggests, the LAD specialises in quick repairs at or near the point of failure, using tools and spares carried by the unit. If the requirement for a longer or more complex repair is diagnosed, the LAD will either call forward a team from the supporting battalion or arrange to have the failed equipment towed to the rear.

SPECIFICATIONS

Type:	armoured recovery vehicle
Manufacturer:	Alvis Vehicles
Powerplant:	Jaguar 4.2-litre petrol
Horsepower:	200
Transmission:	6 + 1
Length:	4.79m (15.71ft)
Width:	2.36m (7.74ft)
Height:	2.25m (7.38ft)
Weight:	8730kg (19,206lb)
Ground clearance:	0.35m (1.14ft)
Armament:	1 x 7.62mm
Crew:	3
Top speed:	72.5km/h (46mph)
Range:	750km (468.75 miles)
Fording:	1.06m (3.47ft)
Gradient:	60 percent
Configuration:	tracked

AARDVARK

The Aardvark Mk4 clears anti-tank and anti-personnel landmines by either detonation or disruption, and is capable of operating in the majority of terrain and environmental conditions encountered in minefields throughout the world. The Mk4 is effective in a variety of soil types and mixes on both flat and undulating ground with gradients of up to 30 percent. It will clear dense surface scrub of 3m (9.84ft) in height and trees with a trunk diameter of 150mm (5.9in), and it will also take out booby traps and trip wires. The cab is a fully armoured structure equipped with 56mm (2.2in) armoured glass windows which are additionally protected by an internal polycarbonate liner and steel grill on the outside. There are facilities for one operator and one additional crew. The inner walls of the crew compartment are lined with a soundproof material and the cab temperature conditions are controlled with heater/air conditioner units. The cab floor has an armour-plated double skin with the lower underside having an angled profile, specifically designed to provide maximum deflection of blast forces. The flail rotor rotates at approximately 300 rounds per minute, with six striker tips striking the ground at any one time, and every piece of ground being struck at least twice.

SPECIFICATIONS

Type:	mine clearer
Manufacturer:	Aardvark Clear Mine Ltd
Powerplant:	New Holland in-line diesel
Horsepower:	160
Transmission:	16 + 16
Length:	8.4m (27.55ft)
Width:	2.53m (8.3ft)
Height:	3.19m (10.46ft)
Weight:	11,506kg (25,313lb)
Ground clearance:	0.38m (1.24ft)
Armament:	none
Crew:	1
Top speed:	20km/h (12.5mph)
Range:	unknown
Fording:	0.5m (1.64ft)
Gradient:	30 percent
Configuration:	semi-tracked

KEILER

The Keiler mine clearer was developed to meet German Army operational requirements regarding the mobility and flexibility of mechanized brigades. The vehicle has been designed to clear a lane of mines 120m (393ft) long, to a depth of 250mm (9.84in) and 4.70m (15.41ft) wide in under 10 minutes. Keiler offers excellent results compared to all other known mine clearing systems, and the crew are under armour protection during all operations. The vehicle can clear both anti-personnel and anti-tank mines in uneven terrain and different soil structures. This is possible because of an onboard sensor control which ensures maximum clearing. Keiler either explodes all mines in front of the vehicle or throws them aside. By means of the cantilever arm, the clearing system is moved from travelling to clearing position, and a tilt and elevation system serves for terrain adjustment. The carrier arm and the clearing shaft frame are driven by hydro-engines. The clearing shaft itself has 24 flails, and is stowed on top of the vehicle while travelling. When ready for operation the clearing shaft is swivelled to the front and locked, with all processes carried out automatically. In total the German Army has ordered 24 Keiler mine clearers, and some have seen service in the former Yugoslavia with UN peacekeeping forces.

SPECIFICATIONS

Type:	mine clearer
Manufacturer:	Rheinmetall
Powerplant:	MTU MB 871 Ka 501
Horsepower:	800
Transmission:	hydro-mechanical
Length:	10.7m (35.1ft)
Width:	6.35m (20.83ft)
Height:	2.76m (9.05ft)
Weight:	53,000kg (116,600lb)
Ground clearance:	0.44m (1.44ft)
Armament:	none
Crew:	2
Top speed:	72km/h (45mph)
Range:	600km (375 miles)
Fording:	1.45m (4.75ft)
Gradient:	60 percent
Configuration:	tracked

M1 MINE CLEARER

The M1 Mine Clearing Blade System is an auxiliary piece of equipment necessary for the tank unit to breach minefields during the normal conduct of operations. In Operation Desert Storm in 1991 track-width mine ploughs proved very successful against pressure-fused anti-tank mines and allowed the M1A1 main battle tank to breach minefields with little loss of momentum. It is electrically operated and is capable of clearing surface or buried mines up to 1.82m (6ft) in front of the tank's path without the aid of supporting forces or additional equipment. In the 1991 Gulf War the M1A1 chassis proved to be fully capable of ploughing, in desert soils, at rates of 30km/h (18.75mph). This chassis, combined with a full-width plough, will provide a full-width breaching capability that will be able to clear all known mines and still be able to manoeuvre with the heavy force. The plough should be fitted with a wire cutter and be capable of ploughing at variable depths, and should be actuated in the centre to allow the blade to be used for digging trails and survivability positions. While this is not its primary mission, it enhances the capabilities of the US Army engineer force. The specifications at right refer to the mine plough only and not the M1 Abrams main battle tank it is attached to.

SPECIFICATIONS

Type:	mine plough
Manufacturer:	Israel Military Industries
Powerplant:	n/a
Horsepower:	n/a
Transmission:	n/a
Ploughing depth:	0.3m (0.98ft)
Ploughed width each side:	1.15m (3.77ft)
Lifted height above ground:	1.6m (5.24ft)
Chain track in centre:	0.71m (2.32ft)
Ground clearance:	n/a
Armament:	n/a
Crew:	n/a
Clearing speed:	6.5km/h (4.06mph)
Range:	n/a
Fording:	n/a
Gradient:	30 percent
Configuration:	n/a

M60 MINE PLOUGH

The M60's mine plough (identical to that fitted on the M1 Abrams) is electrically operated and is capable of clearing surface or buried mines up to 1.82m (6ft) in front of the tank's path without the aid of supporting forces or additional equipment. The adaptation is accomplished by using an adaptor kit and an electrical power interface kit. While the plough is a useful addition to the tank's capabilities, the M60 mine ploughs were found wanting during the 1991 Gulf War, where they proved unable to manoeuvre with US heavy forces due to the inability of the M60 chassis and power train to keep pace with the MIA1 tanks. Engineers also had difficulties associated with maintaining an obsolete, low-density piece of equipment. Many units simply left this equipment behind rather than slow their advance during combat operations. Commanders planned for their use as a part of the deliberate breaching operation of Iraqi defences, but left them behind once they began the pursuit and exploitation phase of the mission. US commanders were unanimous in their opinion that the engineer force needs M1 chassis for heavy breaching and gap-crossing equipment. The specifications at right refer to the mine plough only and not the M60 tank it is attached to.

SPECIFICATIONS

Type:	*mine plough*
Manufacturer:	*Israel Military Industries*
Powerplant:	*n/a*
Horsepower:	*n/a*
Transmission:	*n/a*
Ploughing depth:	*0.3m (0.98ft)*
Ploughed width each side:	*1.15m (3.77ft)*
Lifted height above ground:	*1.6m (5.24ft)*
Chain track in centre:	*0.71m (2.32ft)*
Ground clearance:	*n/a*
Armament:	*n/a*
Crew:	*n/a*
Clearing speed:	*6.5km/h (4.06mph)*
Range:	*n/a*
Fording:	*n/a*
Gradient:	*30 percent*
Configuration:	*n/a*

MINE CLEARER

This vehicle is based on the German Leopard 1 main battle tank chassis, with the turret removed and a new top structure added by the manufacturer, Hägglunds Moelv of Norway. The vehicle is equipped with a flail-based clearing system, external drive system, lane-marking system and an overhead weapons station. The chassis has been modified with an anti-spall liner and mine protection. The new welded top structure has the same armour protection as the rest of the vehicle. The mine-clearing unit itself is mounted on a turntable at the front of the vehicle. The flail system is hydraulically driven and clears a 4m- (13.12ft-) wide safe lane for following tracked vehicles. In transportation mode, the flail is rotated and stored on the top of the vehicle. In operating mode, an external drive system is activated which allows the vehicle to run at a constant speed. As well as the flails, the vehicle can operate the following equipment: explosive mine clearing equipment, electronic mine clearing and detection equipment and a lane-marking system. The vehicle is capable of clearing both anti-tank and anti-personnel, and mines that are both laying on the surface or buried. The forward flails and an armoured body ensure that the two-man crew are fully protected at all times against mine detonation.

SPECIFICATIONS

Type:	mine clearer
Manufacturer:	Hägglunds Moelv AS
Powerplant:	MTU MB 838 Ca M500
Horsepower:	830hp
Transmission:	4 + 2
Length:	9.9m (32.48ft)
Width:	4.8m (15.74ft)
Height:	3m (9.84ft)
Weight:	47,000kg (103,400lb)
Ground clearance:	0.44m (1.44ft)
Armament:	1 x 7.62mm
Crew:	2
Top speed:	65km/h (40.62mph)
Range:	600km (375 miles)
Fording:	4m (13.12ft)
Gradient:	60 percent
Configuration:	tracked

MINE GUZZLER

The Mine Guzzler is based on a double-track arrangement used commercially. A demining roller is carried on hydraulic supports at the front of the vehicle and powered by an engine with hydrostatical drive. The demining roller, which is tiltable to follow ground undulations, is adjustable for depth and has automatic deepholding. It is made up of a series of plates fitted with tungsten carbide teeth which either cause the mines (anti-personnel and anti-tank) to detonate or chew them into small pieces. Damaged plates can easily be replaced by oxyacetylene cutting and welding in the field. Each vehicle has one spare roller to allow the demining work to continue when a roller is under repair. A complete roller change can be effected in less than 30 minutes using the hydraulic supports to lift the roller for access or to load/unload the roller onto a transport vehicle. The Mine Guzzler can clear mines to a depth of 500mm (19.68in) and over a width of 3.2m (10.49ft). Maximum demining speed is 4km/h (2.5mph). The Mine Guzzler may be operated either by remote control, using onboard television cameras, or from the protection of the driver's cabin, which is protected against fragments by a raised armoured superstructure. Mine Guzzler is built to stand detonations from individual explosives up to 12kg (26.4lb) in weight.

SPECIFICATIONS

Type:	demining roller
Manufacturer:	Bofors Defence
Powerplant:	Scania DSI 14 diesel
Horsepower:	500
Transmission:	unknown
Length:	5.3m (17.38ft)
Width:	3.3m (10.82ft)
Height:	3m (9.84ft)
Weight:	45,000kg (99,000lb)
Ground clearance:	0.4m (1.31ft)
Armament:	none
Crew:	1
Top speed:	6.4km/h (4mph)
Range:	unknown
Fording:	unknown
Gradient:	60 percent
Configuration:	tracked

RA-140

This vehicle is designed to clear mines in non-combat conditions, such as humanitarian missions. Although the cabin is armoured it is nowhere near sufficient for in-combat mine clearing. The vehicle is fitted with a 82-chain flail that is powerful enough to destroy the mines (both anti-tank and anti-personnel) before they even detonate. The vehicle is blast-protected and is not damaged even by detonating 10kg (22lb) anti-tank mines. Driving backwards, it clears a path over 3m (9.84ft) wide with a maximum speed of 6km/h (3.75mph) (scatterable mines) or 3km/h (1.87mph) (all other types). The chain rotor consists of 82 chains that whip the ground when rotating, thus detonating or breaking all known mines currently in service. The cabin is completely protected against 7.62mm rounds and against possible shrapnel or fragments from detonating mines or mortar and artillery shells. It is also blast-protected and sound isolated. During transportation the rotor is removed and placed on the vehicle. If the vehicle only has to move a short distance, the rotor is simply lifted hydraulically. The wheels are also bulletproof and mine resistant. The vehicle can be armed with a 12.7mm heavy machine gun, and it also has a camouflage system similar to the one on the XA-180 series.

SPECIFICATIONS

Type:	*mine clearer*
Manufacturer:	*Patria*
Powerplant:	*Deutz, turbocharged, air-cooled*
Horsepower:	*187*
Transmission:	*4 + 1*
Length:	*9.5m (31.16ft)*
Width:	*2.90m (9.51ft)*
Height:	*2.86m (9.38ft)*
Weight:	*15,000kg (33,000lb)*
Ground clearance:	*0.4m (1.31ft)*
Armament:	*1 x 12.7mm*
Crew:	*1*
Top speed:	*70km/h (43.75mph)*
Range:	*250km (156 miles)*
Fording:	*0.8m (2.62ft)*
Gradient:	*60 percent*
Configuration:	*4 x 4*

RHINO

In terms of efficiency, safety, and clearing capacity, the mine clearing system RHINO represents a new generation of large-area mine-clearing systems. Based on well-proven construction machine technology, RHINO offers the maximum in reliability, easy maintenance and servicing. The system was especially developed for humanitarian clearing operations, and consists of an unmanned basic vehicle, a specially designed mine-clearing unit and a mobile control station. Due to RHINO's solid construction and its remote control, optimum safety for the vehicle itself and the crew members during the entire clearing operation is ensured. Even after the detonation of anti-tank mines, the vehicle itself remains undamaged. All material is forced through a gap between two counter-rotating drums. Mines either explode or are destroyed mechanically, so that neither anti-personnel nor anti-tank mines remain intact. The drums are equipped with easy-to-change, long-lasting tungsten carbide chisels. RHINO was delivered to Croatia in August 1998 and has successfully proven its efficiency in all clearing operations of the Croatian demining service. Further RHINO systems were deployed in clearing operations in several countries such as Cambodia, Jordan and South Korea for clearing missions on the border with North Korea.

SPECIFICATIONS

Type:	demining roller
Manufacturer:	Rheinmetall
Powerplant:	Caterpillar diesel
Horsepower:	650
Transmission:	unknown
Length:	9.6m (31.49ft)
Width:	3m (9.84ft)
Height:	3.15m (10.33ft)
Weight:	58,000kg (127,600lb)
Ground clearance:	0.4m (1.31ft)
Armament:	none
Crew:	1
Top speed:	3.8km/h (2.3mph)
Range:	unknown
Fording:	1.2m (3.93ft)
Gradient:	30 percent
Configuration:	tracked

CRUSADER

The Scammell Crusader is essentially a standard civilian vehicle modified to fulfil military requirements. Two basic models were produced, both of which are in service with the British Army. The first, known as the 20-ton tractor, has a two-man cab, and the second, the 35-ton tractor, has a three-man cab. The cab is mounted on the chassis by two rubber-brushed trunnion mountings at the front and two coils sprung with integral telescopic dampers at the rear. The engine is the same in the two models, though the one in the 35-ton model is coupled to an RTO 915 manual gearbox with 15 forward and three reverse gears. Mounted to the rear of the cab is a winch that has a maximum capacity of 8000kg (17,600lb) at a speed of 27.2mm (1.07in) per minute. The winch can be used either to the front or rear and is fitted with an overload warning bell. The front suspension comprises longitudinal semi-elliptical springs; the rear suspension comprises fully articulated, inverted longitudinal semi-elliptical springs. The 20-ton model has 9 forward and 1 reverse gears. Steering is power assisted on both models. The specifications at right refer to the 35 t model. The tyres in the pictures have been prepared for use on snow and ice. This vehicle is in British Army use.

SPECIFICATIONS

Type:	tank transporter
Manufacturer:	Scammell
Powerplant:	Rolls-Royce 305 Mk III
Horsepower:	305
Transmission:	15 + 3
Length:	6.66m (21.85ft)
Width:	2.5m (8.2ft)
Height:	3.3m (10.82ft)
Weight:	11,095kg (24,409ft)
Ground clearance:	0.5m (1.64ft)
Armament:	none
Crew:	1
Top speed:	65km/h (40.62mph)
Range:	500km (312 miles)
Fording:	0.76m (2.49ft)
Gradient:	20 percent
Configuration:	6 x 4

FH16 6 X 6

This emphasis on durability has been a feature of Volvo products ever since the company started operating in 1927. Volvo developed a driven front axle as early as 1937, heralding the birth of Volvo all-wheel drive (AWD). The first Volvo all-wheel drive (AWD) truck was introduced in 1939 in the Swedish army. Since then Volvo has produced more than 30,000 AWD vehicles, from the smallest in today's range, the workhorse in the three- to five-tonne payload model with a six-litre turbocharged diesel engine, to heavy duty, high technology battle-tank transporters with a 16-litre turbocharged diesel engine. The Volvo FH16 6 x 6 is the Volvo heavy tank transporter with a Volvo D16, 16-litre, in-line electrically controlled diesel engine with an output of 520 horsepower at 1800rpm, and equipped with a Volvo EPG engine brake of 374 brake horsepower at 2200rpm. The customer has a choice of the Volvo Powertronic gearbox or an automatic five- or six-speed transmission. In order to utilize the best performance and achieve maximum driveability, the Powertronic can also be equipped with an integrated primary retarder. This gives very high braking power, not only at high speed. Easy tank loading/unloading is done by using two 20-tonne winches that can be manoeuvred separately and at different speeds.

SPECIFICATIONS

Type:	tank transporter
Manufacturer:	Volvo
Powerplant:	D16 16-litre diesel
Horsepower:	520
Transmission:	16 + 1
Length:	7.56m (24.8ft)
Width:	2.5m (8.2ft)
Height:	3.1m (10.17ft)
Weight:	15,000kg (33,000lb)
Ground clearance:	0.4m (1.31ft)
Armament:	none
Crew:	1
Top speed:	80km/h (50mph)
Range:	700km (438 miles)
Fording:	0.5m (1.64ft)
Gradient:	15 percent
Configuration:	6 x 6

M1070

The Heavy Equipment Transporter System (HETS) produced by the Oshkosh Truck Corporation – which consists of the M1070 truck tractor and M1000 semi-trailer – transports tanks and other heavy tracked and wheeled vehicles to and from the battlefield. The M1070 tractor and M1000 semi-trailer replaces the M911/M747 HET system as the US Army's latest model HETS. The M1070/M1000 HETS was developed to accommodate the increased weight of the M1 Abrams family of main battle tanks. The M1070 provides long-haul, local-haul and mainte-nance evacuation on- and offroad during tactical operations worldwide. Unlike previous HETS, the M1070 is designed to carry both the tank and its crew. The HETS is required to transport, deploy and evacuate 70-ton payloads, primarily M-1 tanks, on highways and unimproved roads and cross-country. HETS has automatically steerable axles and load-levelling hydraulic suspension. The tractor has front and rear axle steering with a central tyre inflation system and cab space for five crew members. HETS, which was not available for service during the 1991 Gulf War, entered low-rate ini-tial production soon afterwards. At the completion of the initial contract in 1992, the US Army had purchased 1179 trucks and trailers.

SPECIFICATIONS

Type:	*heavy equipment transporter*
Manufacturer:	*Oshkosh*
Powerplant:	*Detroit Diesel 8V92TA*
Horsepower:	*500*
Transmission:	*5 + 1*
Length:	*9.19m (30.16ft)*
Width:	*2.59m (8.5ft)*
Height:	*3.73m (12.25ft)*
Weight:	*39,009kg (86,000lb)*
Ground clearance:	*0.5m (1.64ft)*
Armament:	*none*
Crew:	*5*
Top speed:	*unknown*
Range:	*520km (325 miles)*
Fording:	*0.71m (2.32ft)*
Gradient:	*15 percent*
Configuration:	*8 x 8*

M1100 WTM

I veco was established in 1975, bringing together the commercial vehicle businesses of Fiat, OM and Lancia Veicoli Speciali in Italy; Unic in France; and Magirus-Deutz in Germany. These mergers created the first truly pan-European truck manufacturer, with a significant presence across all major European markets. In 1986, a joint venture with Ford of Britain led to the creation of Iveco Ford Truck in the United Kingdom and, in 1991, the Spanish company Pegaso and the British Seddon Atkinson joined the group. Iveco has subsequently embarked on one of the most demanding restructuring programmes ever undertaken by a commercial vehicle manufacturer. This rationalization has resulted in Iveco becoming a world leader in transport technology. Iveco Defence Vehicles Division (DVD) is one of the divisions within the Iveco organisation. Iveco DVD has a long history of success in meeting the exacting demands of the military user in the fields of both armoured fighting and logistic vehicles. The M1100 is capable of transporting the Ariete main battle tank. It is a heavy transporter with two winches, each having a pulling capacity of 25,000kg (55,000lb). The 500 horsepower engine is capable of giving the tractor a top speed of 80km/h (50mph), while the front and rear disc brakes provide excellent stopping power.

SPECIFICATIONS

Type:	tank transporter
Manufacturer:	Iveco
Powerplant:	Iveco 8460.41 diesel
Horsepower:	500
Transmission:	16 + 6
Length:	8.64m (28.34ft)
Width:	2.88m (9.44ft)
Height:	3.03m (9.94ft)
Weight:	19,000kg (41,800lb)
Ground clearance:	0.43m (1.41ft)
Armament:	none
Crew:	1
Top speed:	80km/h (50mph)
Range:	unknown
Fording:	1m (3.28ft)
Gradient:	20 percent
Configuration:	8 x 8

T144GB

To pull a trailer loaded with a main battle tank requires a large powerplant. This vehicle is powered by the Environmental class Euro 2 engine. It has a compression ratio of 17:1, maximum power of 530 horsepower at 1900rpm, maximum torque of 2300 and a recommended engine speed of 1200–1550rpm. The size of the engine is 14 litres. Scania has invested heavily in safety for the driver. For example, the seat belt is the single most important item of safety equipment for the driver. With the belt on, the seat occupant stays securely in place instead of risking being catapulted out of the cab. The company has integrated the belt with the seat so that it remains perfectly comfortable even during long stints behind the wheel. Additional protection is available in the form of a belt pre-tensioner and airbag, but for these features to be effective, the seat belt must be worn. Scania trucks feature an under-run beam in the front bumper as standard. This considerably increases the survival margin in crashes. Scania offers electronically regulated disc brakes on most models in long-haul and distribution operations. Disc brakes offer extra-high braking power and reduce the risk of brake fade, while the electronic brake regulation system increases the speed and precision of brake operation. This vehicle is in Belgian Army service.

SPECIFICATIONS

Type:	tank transporter
Manufacturer:	Scania
Powerplant:	Enviromental class Euro 2 diesel
Horsepower:	530
Transmission:	9 + 1
Length:	8.2m (26.9ft)
Width:	2.49m (8.16ft)
Height:	3.44m (11.28ft)
Weight:	38,500kg (84,700lb)
Ground clearance:	0.31m (1.01m)
Armament:	none
Crew:	1
Top speed:	80km/h (50mph)
Range:	unknown
Fording:	0.5m (1.64ft)
Gradient:	30 percent
Configuration:	6 x 4

T-815

The TATRA T815-24EN34 semi-trailer prime mover is designed to haul semi-trailers transporting tanks, armoured personnel carriers and other military loads. The 6 x 6 all-wheel drive uses the TATRA-designed suspension system – central backbone tube with swing half-axles – which is extremely resistant against torsional and bending stresses and makes it possible to negotiate difficult terrain and rough surfaces at higher speeds. It also gives better ride comfort than with a conventional chassis. This semi-trailer also incorporates airbags and leaf springs, which makes it possible to keep the fifth wheel height independent of the load. The braking system comprises dual-circuit pressure air brakes, which are load sensitive and act on the wheels of all the axles. The emergency brake is a spring type which acts on the rear axle wheels only. The vehicle has 10 forward and 2 reverse gears and, except for the first and reverse gears, all gears are synchronized. The cab is all metal with a hydraulic tilt and two doors. Inside are two full-size seats and an emergency seat which can be adapted into a berth should the need arise. The steering is left-hand drive with integral power assistance, and the clutch is single plate with a diaphragm spring.

SPECIFICATIONS

Type:	*prime mover*
Manufacturer:	*TATRA*
Powerplant:	*TATRA T3B92B*
Horsepower:	*400*
Transmission:	*10 + 2*
Length:	*7.6m (24.93ft)*
Width:	*2.5m (8.2ft)*
Height:	*3.03m (9.94ft)*
Weight:	*36,000kg (79,200lb)*
Ground clearance:	*0.35m(1.14ft)*
Armament:	*none*
Crew:	*1*
Top speed:	*80km/h (50mph)*
Range:	*400km (250 miles)*
Fording:	*0.4m (1.31ft)*
Gradient:	*22 percent*
Configuration:	*6 x 6*

40.10

The Iveco 40.10 light truck, currently in use with the Italian Army, has a conventional layout with the engine at the front and the cargo area at the rear. Having a payload of 1500kg (3300lb), it is ideally suited for many tactical roles such as troop and cargo carrier. The driving cab usually has a soft canvas top though a hard top is also available. The cargo compartment is of all-steel construction and has folding seats along each side for 10 men. The bonnet can be removed to allow access to the engine for routine maintenance. The truck can be configured in a number of ways. For example, a van body is available as well as a four-stretcher ambulance body. The cargo area can also house numerous weapons, such as the 106mm recoilless rifle, plus anti-tank weapons, machine guns and rocket launchers. The truck itself can tow a 105mm light artillery piece, and an optional front winch is also available. Two 40.10 trucks can be fitted inside a C-130 Hercules transport aircraft for rapid deployment, and a stripped-down one can be accommodated inside a C-223 transport aircraft. The axles are of the single reduction type front and rear, both with locking differentials. Hydraulic power steering is standard and left- and right-hand steering versions are available.

SPECIFICATIONS

Type:	light truck
Manufacturer:	Iveco
Powerplant:	Fiat 8142 diesel
Horsepower:	103
Transmission:	5 + 1
Length:	4.64m (15.22ft)
Width:	2m (6.56ft)
Height:	2.38m (7.8ft)
Weight:	4300kg (9460lb)
Ground clearance:	0.4m (1.31ft)
Armament:	none
Crew:	1
Top speed:	100km/h (62.5mph)
Range:	500km (312 miles)
Fording:	0.7m (2.29ft)
Gradient:	60 percent
Configuration:	4 x 4

ATMP

Supacat has been in service with the British Army since the mid-1980s as an all-terrain mobile platform. It is a fully automatic 6 x 6 airportable and amphibious vehicle, with a 1000kg (2200lb) payload and an unrivalled all-terrain capability. The Mark III version has recently been selected by Great Britain's Ministry of Defence for the British Army's 16th Air Assault Brigade as part of the All Terrain Mobile Platform (ATMP) programme. The vehicle uses a forward-controlling driving position with accommodation for a passenger next to the driver and space for a further four men in the rear if necessary. The vehicle has a limited amphibious capability and can also travel through snow. However, in arctic conditions tracks can be fitted to make transport easier – they take around 15 minutes to fit. As well as an all-terrain vehicle, it is possible that the ATMP can be used as an anti-tank and anti-aircraft missile carrier. A specially designed transporter trailer which tilts automatically for loading and off-loading is also available. The payload for the vehicle is 1000kg (2200lb), and with the trailer this increases by a further 400kg (880lb). The ATMP may be used in an all-flat bed form or with a fixed cab depending on mission requirements.

SPECIFICATIONS

Type:	*light vehicle*
Manufacturer:	*Alvis Vehicles*
Powerplant:	*VW 1.588 diesel*
Horsepower:	*54*
Transmission:	*3 + 1*
Length:	*3.14m (10.3ft)*
Width:	*2m (6.56ft)*
Height:	*2m (6.56ft)*
Weight:	*2520kg (5544lb)*
Ground clearance:	*0.24m (0.78ft)*
Armament:	*none*
Crew:	*1*
Top speed:	*48km/h (30mph)*
Range:	*unknown*
Fording:	*0.75m (2.46ft)*
Gradient:	*45 percent*
Configuration:	*6 x 6*

AWB BEDFORD

This truck was the winner of the British Army's 4 x 4000kg (8800lb) truck competition to replace the venerable Bedford RL truck. The vehicle has a ladder-type chassis with six cross-members, two being of "alligator jaw" design. The two-door forward control cab is of all-steel construction and has a circular observation hatch in the roof. Access to the engine is via the top-hinged panels on the rear of the cab at either side, and the cab between the driver's and passenger's seats is easily removed for access to the engine. The rear cargo area has drop tail-gate and sides, which can be removed easily for the stowage of containers. A hydraulic crane can be fitted for unloading, and detachable outward-facing seats can be fitted in the centre of the cargo area for the transport of passengers. This ubiquitous vehicle comes in a number of variants: dump truck, refueller and portable roadway laying vehicle. The Bedford can also be fitted with a winch, which has a capacity of 5080kg (11,176lb) and a cable length of 76m (249.3ft). The cab itself can be made mineproof, though this requires detailed work carried out by specialist firm. Some 50,000 Bedfords have been manufactured, testimony to its robust and reliable qualities.

SPECIFICATIONS

Type:	4000kg truck
Manufacturer:	AWB Bedford
Powerplant:	Bedford 5.42 diesel
Horsepower:	98
Transmission:	4 + 1
Length:	6.57m (21.55ft)
Width:	2.48m (8.13ft)
Height:	3.4m (11.15ft)
Weight:	11,180kg (24,596lb)
Ground clearance:	0.34m (1.11ft)
Armament:	none
Crew:	1
Top speed:	77km/h (48.12mph)
Range:	560km (350 miles)
Fording:	0.76m (2.49ft)
Gradient:	49 percent
Configuration:	4 x 4

BV206

The Bv206 all-terrain carrier is a family of multipurpose amphibious tracked vehicles. The Bv206 can be found in both military and civilian applications all over the world and new categories of users appear all the time. From the earliest stage, the Bv206 was designed to be versatile and it has been proven so in service. With generous power driving on all four of the tracks, which exert a ground pressure of less than half of a man's foot, the Bv206 can negotiate such obstacles as soft snow, drifting sand and marshlands. It can climb considerable gradients, swim without preparation and work in arctic cold or in tropical heat. The load capacity is 2250kg (4950lb). A trailer of 2500kg (5500lb) gross weight can also be towed. The front and rear units are connected by a unique hydraulic steering linkage, which gives great flexibility in all axles and extremely good manoeuvrability. The simplicity in the handling of the vehicle involves a minimum of driver training. The vehicle can be airdropped and transported by a variety of aircraft and helicopters. The latest member of the Bv206 family is the improved armoured version called BvS10. The BvS10 is a new larger vehicle, with improved load capacity. The BvS10 has the same superior mobility in difficult terrain as the Bv206, combined with the same speed on road.

SPECIFICATIONS

Type:	all-terrain carrier
Manufacturer:	Hägglunds
Powerplant:	Mercedes OM 603.950
Horsepower:	136
Transmission:	4 + 1
Length:	6.9m (22.63ft)
Width:	1.87m (6.13ft)
Height:	2.3m (7.54ft)
Weight:	4500kg (9900lb)
Ground clearance:	0.35m (1.14ft)
Armament:	none
Crew:	1
Top speed:	52km/h (32.5mph)
Range:	330km (206 miles)
Fording:	amphibious
Gradient:	60 percent
Configuration:	tracked

DROPS

The Demountable Rack Offload and Pickup System (DROPS) is currently in use with the British Army. The Leyland DAF is an 8 x 6 vehicle that can carry a 15,000kg (33,000lb) payload with a mobility equivalent to a medium load, hence its name Medium Mobility Load Carrier (MMLC). It uses a forward control cab with seating for the driver and a second crew member; there is also space for a third crew member if necessary, plus space for crew stowage. A hatch with a machine-gun mounting is located in the roof (which can take the weight of two men). The vehicle uses the Multilift Mark 4 load-handling system, which was designed for offroad military applications. The control system uses automatic single lever operation with two modes of backup for emergencies. It allows the carrier vehicle not only to lift flatracks onto the carrier but also to move them on the ground. The driver controls the hook arm, which lowers and then lifts the flatrack onto the vehicle. Load and unload times are between 25 and 30 seconds. The system uses a simple chassis interface with minimum mounting points and high-quality steel throughout. All pivots and bearings are designed for ease of access, including grease seals.

SPECIFICATIONS

Type:	*logistic support*
Manufacturer:	*Leyland DAF*
Powerplant:	*Eagle 350M diesel*
Horsepower:	*350*
Transmission:	*6 + 1*
Length:	*9.11m (29.88ft)*
Width:	*2.5m (8.2ft)*
Height:	*3.18m (10.43ft)*
Weight:	*32,000kg (70,400lb)*
Ground clearance:	*0.28m (0.91ft)*
Armament:	*none*
Crew:	*2*
Top speed:	*75km/h (46.87mph)*
Range:	*500km (312 miles)*
Fording:	*0.75m (2.46ft)*
Gradient:	*61 percent*
Configuration:	*8 x 6*

FM12

The Volvo FM12 is a powerful, robust truck built for very demanding duties and is certified for gross combination weights of up to 100,000kg (220,000lb) in heavy construction work. The Volvo FM12 has a raised ground clearance, low-loading height, well-protected components and Powertronic or I-shift automatic gearboxes. Safety features include the Electronic Stability Programme (ESP), which activates the braking system automatically if the truck shows tendencies to abnormal behaviour. Electronically controlled disc brakes on air suspended models minimize the risk of brake fade, and a computerized driver information system with large display for driver information gives clear feedback on the truck's functions and status. Brake blending ensures that the disc brakes, retarder and/or Volvo Engine Brake interact to provide optimum braking. Driver comfort is improved by ergonomically designed and logically grouped instruments. Comfortable, air-suspended seats with adjustable damping and integrated seat belts, available with the option of built-in heating and ventilation, are also available. The cab is easy to tilt either manually or with the help of the optional electrically powered hydraulic pump. A cab tilt angle of 70 degrees allows easy access to most service components.

SPECIFICATIONS

Type:	*heavy truck*
Manufacturer:	*Volvo*
Powerplant:	*D12C 420 diesel*
Horsepower:	*414*
Transmission:	*6 + 1*
Length:	*8.45m (27.72ft)*
Width:	*2.46m (8.07ft)*
Height:	*2.86m (9.38ft)*
Weight:	*35,000kg (77,000lb)*
Ground clearance:	*0.23m (0.75ft)*
Armament:	*none*
Crew:	*1*
Top speed:	*80km/h (50mph)*
Range:	*500km (312 miles)*
Fording:	*1.1m (3.6ft)*
Gradient:	*30 percent*
Configuration:	*6 x 6*

HEMTT

The M977 Series of Heavy Expanded Mobility Tactical Trucks (HEMTT) is considered by many to be the world's premier heavy duty tactical truck, and was affectionately referred to as "The Ship of the Desert" during the 1991 Gulf War. The 8 x 8 HEMTT is highly valued for its ability to provide support wherever the US Army's tanks are going. Over 15,000 HEMTTs have been built and fielded since 1982, with the newest model, the HEMTT Load Handling System (LHS), now entering production to support transportation of palletized loads. The HEMTT Overhaul programme is the systematic disassembly, component rebuild and production-line truck re-assembly providing the same performance, life-span and warranty as a new HEMTT. Of the 15,000 HEMTTs built by Oshkosh, over 800 have been overhauled to date. There are five basic configurations of the HEMTT series trucks: M977 cargo truck with Material Handling Crane (MHC), M978 2500-gallon fuel tanker, M984 wrecker, M983 tractor and M985 cargo truck with MHC. A self-recovery winch is also available on certain models. This vehicle family is rapidly deployable and is designed to operate in any climatic condition where military operations are expected to occur.

SPECIFICATIONS

Type:	heavy truck
Manufacturer:	Oshkosh
Powerplant:	DDC Model 8V92TA
Horsepower:	450
Transmission:	4-speed automatic
Length:	10.17m (33.36ft)
Width:	2.43m (7.97ft)
Height:	2.56m (8.39ft)
Weight:	28,123kg (62,000lb)
Ground clearance:	0.6m (1.96ft)
Armament:	none
Crew:	1
Top speed:	62mph (38.75mph)
Range:	640km (400 miles)
Fording:	0.12m (0.39ft)
Gradient:	60 percent
Configuration:	8 x 8

LAND ROVER 90

The Land Rover 90 is fitted with long-travel coil spring suspension and front disc brakes. It has a boxed-section steel chassis with a cross member bolted in place to aid removal of the gearbox and transfer box. Suspension movement is controlled at the front and the rear by long-stroke hydraulic dampers. The front beam axle is located by radius arms with Panhard rods providing lateral location. The rear axle is located by tubular trailing links with a centrally mounted A-frame. Up to three engines are available for this vehicle: 2.5-litre petrol, 3.5-litre V-8 petrol and a 2.5-litre diesel, which is available in naturally aspirated or turbocharged versions. The gearbox and transfer in the 90 is the same as those in the 110. Like all Land Rover vehicles, the 90 comes with a number of options, including open top with folding windscreen and detachable door tops, a roll-over bar, NATO standard towing jaw and 12-pin trailer socket, blackout lighting systems, small-arms clips, hand throttle, wire mesh lamp guards, raised air intake, and front and rear seating options. Land Rover vehicles are popular around the world and are manufactured in many countries, including Australia, Malaysia, Turkey, Zambia, Morocco and Zaire.

SPECIFICATIONS

Type:	light vehicle
Manufacturer:	Land Rover
Powerplant:	V-8 petrol
Horsepower:	134
Transmission:	5 + 1
Length:	3.72m (12.2ft)
Width:	1.79m (5.87ft)
Height:	1.99m (6.52ft)
Weight:	2550kg (5610lb)
Ground clearance:	0.21m (0.68ft)
Armament:	depends on variant
Crew:	1
Top speed:	105km/h (65.62mph)
Range:	600km (375 miles)
Fording:	0.5m (1.64ft)
Gradient:	39 percent
Configuration:	4 x 4

LAND ROVER 110

The 110 is based on a box-section steel chassis used on the civilian Range Rover, though considerably strengthened. This strength has been incorporated to allow the vehicle to withstand the most demanding offroad conditions. The suspension uses coil springs in place of the earlier leaf-spring type. The military version of the 110 is in service with the British Army and is known by the designation Truck, Utility, Medium. A wide range of conversions have been developed for this vehicle, including a special forces patrol vehicle, armoured patrol vehicle, mobile workshops, shelter vehicles, ambulances, towlift recovery vehicles and a hydraulically operated multi-loader. Weapons fit depends on the version, but can include MILAN anti-tank rocket launcher, 70mm multiple rocket system and 7.62mm machine guns. Factory fitted options include truck cab, open top with folding windscreen and detachable door tops, rollover bar, additional fuel tanks, air conditioning, small-arms clips, wire mesh lamp guards, disruptive-pattern camouflage paint, cabinets for jerry can stowage, and external pick and shovel stowage. The popularity of Land Rover vehicles stems from their versatility, ruggedness and ease of maintenance in the field, which often involves nothing more than work with a hammer and screwdriver.

SPECIFICATIONS

Type:	lightweight vehicle
Manufacturer:	Land Rover
Powerplant:	V-8 watercooled petrol
Horsepower:	134
Transmission:	5 + 1
Length:	4.63m (15.19ft)
Width:	1.79m (5.87ft)
Height:	1.03m (3.37ft)
Weight:	3050kg (6710lb)
Ground clearance:	0.21m (0.68ft)
Armament:	depends on variant
Crew:	1
Top speed:	105km/h (65.62mph)
Range:	600km (375 miles)
Fording:	0.7m (2.29ft)
Gradient:	40 percent
Configuration:	4 x 4

LEYLAND DAF

C urrently in service with the British Army following the award by the Ministry of Defence of a production contract to Leyland DAF in 1989, this truck is conventional in both layout and design. The sleeper cab has room for the driver, two passengers and stowage for their kit. Alternatively, the space can be used for driver training or radio communications equipment depending on the requirement. The cab roof itself is strengthened to bear the weight of two men and has provision for a roof hatch and machine-gun installation over an observer's platform inside the cab. There are a number of fitments that can be added to the truck, including front-end rotating hooks, lugs for suspended or supported recovery and an infrared reflective paint finish. The body has been designed to accommodate interchange-able drop sides, a tailboard and canopy. Options include left- or right-hand drive, a winch, hydraulic crane, tipping body or a chassis-and-cab-only arrangement. The front axle has a rating of 4850kg (10,670lb) with an off-set bowl to reduce cab height, and the rear axle has a rating of 6800kg (14,960lb). The vehicle can accommodate numerous items of military equipment, such as NATO-standard pallets, containers and fuel pods.

SPECIFICATIONS

Type:	medium truck
Manufacturer:	Leyland DAF
Powerplant:	Leyland DAF 310 diesel
Horsepower:	145
Transmission:	5 + 1
Length:	6.65m (21.81ft)
Width:	2.49m (8.16ft)
Height:	3.43m (11.25ft)
Weight:	10,800kg (23,760lb)
Ground clearance:	0.32m (1.04ft)
Armament:	none
Crew:	1
Top speed:	89km/h (55.62mph)
Range:	500km (312 miles)
Fording:	0.75m (2.46ft)
Gradient:	33 percent
Configuration:	4 x 4

M115.18WM

The success Iveco has enjoyed is due to a process of continuous product evolution, which means that the specification and choice of models are always being changed to meet the needs of military customers. The latest evolution is the range of medium trucks. The M115 has been designed to be more responsive, more reliable and more profitable for customers. In addition to boasting the pedigree of a truck that has already won more awards than any other, it has now been equipped with a new engine offering even higher standards of productivity. The new Tector engine has been designed specifically for the EuroCargo by Iveco, one of the world's largest manufacturers of truck diesel engines. The new Tector engine family is in fact the latest in a generation of leading edge engines, specifically designed by Iveco. The advent of the unprecedented "common rail" direct injection diesel turbo engines with four valves per cylinder and integrated intake manifold offers new levels of reliability, long-term durability and low impact on the environment. The fascia is ergonomical, the instrumentation is housed in an anti-glare dashboard, and the main controls are on the three steering column stalks. The large side windows, extending below the waistline, provide excellent kerbside vision.

SPECIFICATIONS

Type:	medium truck
Manufacturer:	Iveco
Powerplant:	Iveco Tector diesel
Horsepower:	177
Transmission:	6 + 1
Length:	6.96m (22.83ft)
Width:	2.48m (8.13ft)
Height:	3.07m (10.07ft)
Weight:	12,400kg (27,280ft)
Ground clearance:	0.43m (1.41ft)
Armament:	none
Crew:	1
Top speed:	80km/h (50mph)
Range:	500km (312 miles)
Fording:	unknown
Gradient:	60 percent
Configuration:	4 x 4

M150.30WM

Besides vehicle performance, cost effective logistic and after-sales support are key drivers in Iveco's design philosophy for military customers. Maximum use of commercial off-the-shelf components with proven reliability contributes to lower life-cycle costs as well as minimizing the cost of replacement parts. Computerized diagnostic systems for maintenance and fleet management are provided, essential tools for ensuring long and efficient vehicle life. Iveco fits a number of useful features into its machines. For example, fully electronic engine management is by means of an engine control unit (ECU) fitted directly to the engine via a connecting plate in which fuel is circulated to cool it down. To facilitate diagnostic tasks, the ECU memorizes several operating parameters, such as coolant temperature, oil temperature and pressure, as well as any instance of malfunctioning. In the event of a failure, Iveco has designed a feature that facilitates return to base: the computer will see to the engine's "self-defence" by activating a "limp-home" programme that makes it possible to keep working with downgraded performance capabilities. If necessary, the data saved can be transmitted to the Iveco service network via a cable or via the telecommunications lines.

SPECIFICATIONS

Type:	heavy truck
Manufacturer:	Iveco
Powerplant:	Iveco CURSOR 8 diesel
Horsepower:	221
Transmission:	16 + 16 or 5 + 5
Length:	7.87m (25.82ft)
Width:	2.5m (8.2ft)
Height:	3m (9.84ft)
Weight:	17,000kg (37,400lb)
Ground clearance:	0.43m (1.41ft)
Armament:	none
Crew:	1
Top speed:	90km/h (56.25mph)
Range:	500km (312 miles)
Fording:	unknown
Gradient:	60 percent
Configuration:	4 x 4

M250.37WM

The cab of the M250 is modelled on the civilian road versions of the model; it therefore offers the driver a comfortable and ergonomic working environment. Iveco has invested a lot of time and money in cab design, and that's why the EuroTrakker Cursor results in an even more comfortable cab, in which insulation has been improved by 20 percent and soundproofing has been reduced. Working in difficult conditions is no longer a problem, the Eurotrakker Cursor uses a new cab suspension system, capable of isolating the driver from the ruggedness of the terrain and of softening rolling on bends, giving greater driving comfort. What's more, to ensure value is retained over time, the cab panels are galvanized on both sides. This guarantees greater protection and durability for the driver compartment. Like the rest of their military range, this vehicle is powered by an Iveco engine. Four million engines currently operate on various types of machine, from the simplest to the most complex, guaranteeing customers a high level of reliability and durability that is the outcome of Iveco's long tradition in engine production. Iveco engines are ideal for the military market because they have long intervals between overhauls. This means that they can support military operations for extended lengths of time.

SPECIFICATIONS

Type:	heavy truck
Manufacturer:	Iveco
Powerplant:	Iveco 8460.41 diesel
Horsepower:	272
Transmission:	6 + 6
Length:	8.59m (28.18ft)
Width:	2.5m (8.2ft)
Height:	3m (9.84ft)
Weight:	25,000kg (55,000lb)
Ground clearance:	0.43m (1.41ft)
Armament:	none
Crew:	1
Top speed:	90km/h (56.25mph)
Range:	500km (312 miles)
Fording:	unknown
Gradient:	60 percent
Configuration:	6 x 6

M320.42WM

Like most Iveco transport vehicles, the M320 uses ABS as standard and the front axles of partial drive versions are equipped with disc brakes, while the drive axles are equipped with drum brakes. Some of the advantages of the front disc brakes are: balancing of brake power (left and right), rapid reaction times, and quick and easy substitution of brake pads. All of this means an increase in safety and a reduction in operating costs. The efficiency of the brake system is improved by not only the ABS system, but also the EBL (Electronic Braking Limitation) system, an electronic braking corrector integrated into the ABS system, which requires no servicing interventions at all. The Air Processing Unit (APU) system also adds to the reliability of the brake system components as it improves the air-drying process through an air heating and filtering system which feeds the whole pneumatic system. Iveco supplies the Italian Army with its range of trucks, and also the Ariete main battle tank. Like most Iveco vehicles, the M320 is C-130 transportable and the cab area is easily armoured with the addition of appliqué panels. This means that the vehicle can withstand hits from small-arms fire and artillery fragments, thereby allowing it to operate near the frontline if necessary.

SPECIFICATIONS

Type:	heavy truck
Manufacturer:	Iveco
Powerplant:	Iveco CURSOR 10 diesel
Horsepower:	420
Transmission:	6 + 6
Length:	10.15m (33.3ft)
Width:	2.5m (8.2ft)
Height:	3.34m (10.95ft)
Weight:	32,000kg (70,400lb)
Ground clearance:	0.43m (1.41ft)
Armament:	none
Crew:	1
Top speed:	90km/h (56.25mph)
Range:	450km (281 miles)
Fording:	unknown
Gradient:	60
Configuration:	8 x 8

M809

The M809 series of trucks in service with the US Army is similar to the older M54 series, with a diesel engine fitted in place of the multi-fuel powerplant of the earlier model. Production of the M809 started in 1970 and by the mid-1980s AM General had built 38,000 vehicles. The chassis consists of two rail-type beams with six reinforced cross-members. The layout of the truck is conventional: the engine at the front, a two-door cab in the centre with a windscreen that can be folded flat against the bonnet, a removable canvas top and a cargo compartment at the rear. The basic cargo variant has an all-steel rear cargo body with drop sides, removable bows, tarpaulin cover and troop seats down either side for up to 18 fully equipped troops. A number of extras are available for this vehicle, including A-frame, air brakes, closure hard-top, deep water fording, thermal barrier and water personnel heater. In addition, a winch can be fitted at the front. The trucks can also be fitted with the Enhanced Mobility System for increased mobility over sand, snow and mud. The truck is in the service of the US Army and several other armed forces around the world, including Jordan, South Korea, Pakistan and Thailand. As can be seen in the photograph, equipment can also be stashed on the cab roof.

SPECIFICATIONS

Type:	cargo truck
Manufacturer:	AM General
Powerplant:	NHC-250 diesel
Horsepower:	240
Transmission:	5 + 1
Length:	7.65m (25.09ft)
Width:	2.46m (8.07ft)
Height:	2.94m (8.16ft)
Weight:	18,985kg (41,767lb)
Ground clearance:	0.29m (0.95ft)
Armament:	none
Crew:	1
Top speed:	84km/h (52.5mph)
Range:	563km (352 miles)
Fording:	0.76m (2.49ft)
Gradient:	67 percent
Configuration:	6 x 6

M923

The M923 is a dropside version of the venerable M939 series of 6 x 6 cargo trucks in US service. The truck has a fully automatic transmission that eliminates over-revving, is very reliable, easy to operate and features improvements in overall safety. For example, the driver controls the engagement of the front wheels for 6 x 6 drive with an air system, which eliminates the need for a mechanical sprague clutch, which often failed. The truck is equipped with air brakes, which are self-adjusting and are backed by fail-safe mechanical spring brakes. The front-mounted winch is hydraulically driven and stops when overloaded and restarts when the overload is removed. The bonnet and bumpers tilt forward to allow maintenance to be carried out from ground level. Flat tyres are replaced using a boom positioned just behind the cab. In April 1981 the AM Corporation was awarded a contract for 11,394 M939s, later increased to 22,789. AM General completed its five-year contract in September 1986, though production was extended until April 1987 by the award of a further contract for 1107 vehicles. As a result of this large production run the M939 series is in widespread use. There is no doubt that this series of trucks has been the backbone of the US Army for over 20 years.

SPECIFICATIONS

Type:	cargo truck
Manufacturer:	AM General
Powerplant:	Cummins NHC-250 diesel
Horsepower:	240
Transmission:	5 + 1
Length:	7.74m (25.39ft)
Width:	2.46m (8.07ft)
Height:	2.94m (9.64ft)
Weight:	9797kg (21,553lb)
Ground clearance:	0.27m (0.88ft)
Armament:	none
Crew:	1
Top speed:	84km/h (52.5mph)
Range:	563km (352 miles)
Fording:	0.76m (2.49ft)
Gradient:	60 percent
Configuration:	6 x 6

M939A2

The story of this vehicle begins with the earlier M809 series of 6 x 6 trucks that was developed and produced by the AM General Corporation. Production began in 1970, and by mid-1980 some 38,000 vehicles had been completed. The company announced in 1988 that it was withdrawing from the manufacture of medium and heavy vehicles. However, the US Army awarded an engineering contract to AM General for the further development of the M809, which resulted in the M939. In April 1979 AM was awarded a contract for 11,394 M939s, later increased to 22,789. In May 1986 ARVECO, a joint venture between BMY Corporation and the General Automotive Company, was awarded a contract to build 15,218 M939A2s over a five-year period. The first deliveries were made in early 1987. The M939 is essentially the M809 with improved transmission, transfer case and braking system. The M939A2 incorporates a central tyre inflation system. The powerplant is the Cummins engine producing 240 horsepower at 2100 revolutions per minute and giving the vehicle a range of 644km (402 miles). There are a number of kits for the M939 series, including automatic chemical alarm, deep water fording, bow and tarpaulin cover, electric brake, engine coolant heater and hard-top closure.

SPECIFICATIONS

Type:	cargo truck
Manufacturer:	BMY Division of HARSCO
Powerplant:	Cummins NHC-250 diesel
Horsepower:	240
Transmission:	5 + 1
Length:	7.74m (25.39ft)
Width:	2.46m (8.07ft)
Height:	2.94m (9.64ft)
Weight:	9797kg (21,553lb)
Ground clearance:	0.27m (0.88ft)
Armament:	none
Crew:	1
Top speed:	84km/h (52.5mph)
Range:	644km (402 miles)
Fording:	0.76m (2.49ft)
Gradient:	60 percent
Configuration:	6 x 6

M998

The High Mobility Multi-purpose Wheeled Vehicle (HMMWV) is the replacement vehicle for the M151 series of jeeps. Its mission is to provide a light tactical vehicle for command and control, special-purpose shelter carriers, and special-purpose weapons platforms throughout all areas of the modern battlefield. It is supported using the current logistics and maintenance structure established for US Army wheeled vehicles. The HMMWV is equipped with a high-performance diesel engine, automatic transmission and four wheel drive and is air transportable and droppable from a variety of aircraft. The HMMWV can be equipped with a self-recovery winch and can support payloads from 1136kg to 2000kg (2500lb to 4400lb) depending on the model. The family includes utility/cargo, shelter carrier, armament carrier, ambulance, anti-tank missile carrier and scout reconnaissance configuration. A basic armour package is standard on the Armament and anti-tank missile carrier models. A more heavily armoured, or Up-Armour, HMMWV is now being produced in limited quantities, primarily for the Scout Platoon application. Special supplemental armour versions have been developed for USMC requirements (unique model numbers designate these configurations).

SPECIFICATIONS

Type:	utility vehicle
Manufacturer:	AM General
Powerplant:	V8, 6.2 litre diesel
Horsepower:	150
Transmission:	3-speed automatic
Length:	4.57m (14.99ft)
Width:	2.16m (7.08ft)
Height:	1.83m (6ft)
Weight:	2363kg (5200lb)
Ground clearance:	0.4m (1.33ft)
Armament:	depends on configuration
Crew:	2–4
Top speed:	88km/h (55mph)
Range:	560km (350 miles)
Fording:	0.76m (2.5ft)
Gradient:	60 percent
Configuration:	4 x 4

M1078

Stewart & Stevenson Tactical Vehicle Systems, LP (TVSLP), a segment of Stewart & Stevenson Services, Inc. (NASDAQ: SSSS), is the manufacturer and prime contractor of the Family of Medium Tactical Vehicles (FMTV) for the US Army. The M1078 Standard Cargo Truck is designed to transport cargo and soldiers. The M1078 has a payload capacity of 2272kg (5000lb), and to facilitate loading/unloading the bed-side rails are mounted on hinges and can be lowered. The cargo bed can be equipped with an optional bench seat kit for the transport of soldiers. The bench seats are constructed of a non-wood material and attach to the cargo bed side rails, and can be folded down and stowed when not in use. Soldiers are assisted when climbing in and out of the cargo bed area with the aid of a ladder, which is stowed on the vehicle when not in use. A canvas and bows kit is available to keep both soldiers and cargo protected from the elements. The M1078 can be equipped with an optional electrically operated self-recovery winch kit capable of fore and aft vehicle recovery operations. The winch has a lift capacity of 682kg (1500lb). The winch has 93.87m (308ft) of line capacity and 4545kg (10,000lb) bare drum line pull at 110 percent overload.

SPECIFICATIONS

Type:	medium truck
Manufacturer:	Stewart & Stevenson
Powerplant:	Caterpillar, 6.6l diesel
Horsepower:	225
Transmission:	7-speed automatic
Length:	6.42m (21ft)
Width:	2.43m (7.97ft)
Height:	2.84m (9.31ft)
Weight:	7484kg (16,465lb)
Ground clearance:	0.55m (1.8ft)
Armament:	none
Crew:	1
Top speed:	94km/h (58.75mph)
Range:	645km (403 miles)
Fording:	0.91m (2.98ft)
Gradient:	60 percent
Configuration:	4 x 4

M1079

The Family of Medium Tactical Vehicles (FMTVs) was first produced and fielded to US Army units in 1996. This family of vehicles was designed to improve upon and replace the ageing fleet of medium tactical vehicles. The FMTVs are based on a common truck cab and chassis. The Light Medium Tactical Vehicle (LMTV) designates the 2-tonne payload capacity models consisting of cargo, airdrop cargo, and van models. The Medium Tactical Vehicle (MTV) designates the 5-ton payload capacity models consisting of cargo with and without Material Handling Equipment (MHE), airdrop cargo, long wheelbase cargo with and without MHE, tractor, wrecker, dump and airdrop dump. The M1079 van is designed to be used as a mobile shop by Direct Support Unit Maintenance contact teams. The M1079 van body is constructed of aluminium and is equipped with three double-paned windows, blackout shields, double rear doors, removable steps, and an AC/DC electrical junction box and multiple outlets. The van body can be equipped with heater and/or air conditioner. The M1079 can be equipped with a self-recovery winch kit capable of fore and aft vehicle recovery operations. It has the same characteristics as the M1078 truck's winch (see page 77).

SPECIFICATIONS

Type:	*medium van*
Manufacturer:	*Stewart & Stevenson*
Powerplant:	*Caterpillar 6.6-litre diesel*
Horsepower:	*225*
Transmission:	*7-speed automatic*
Length:	*6.7m (21.98ft)*
Width:	*2.43m (7.97ft)*
Height:	*3.48m (11.41ft)*
Weight:	*8156kg (17,943lb)*
Ground clearance:	*0.55m (1.8ft)*
Armament:	*none*
Crew:	*1*
Top speed:	*94km/h (58.75mph)*
Range:	*645km (403 miles)*
Fording:	*0.91m (2.98ft)*
Gradient:	*60 percent*
Configuration:	*4 x 4*

M1085

Deployability, maintainability, versatility, mobility and agility are some of the words that describe the US Army's transformation. They're also words that describe the FMTV, a critical enabler for the US Army's future vision of a more deployable and lethal combat force. The M1085 Long Wheel Base (LWB) Truck is designed to transport soldiers and cargo in International Standardized Operations Containers. The M1085 has a payload capacity of 4545kg (10,000lb) and to facilitate loading/unloading, the bed side rails are mounted on hinges. The cargo bed can be equipped with an optional bench seat kit for transport of soldiers. The bench seats are constructed of a non-wood material and attach to the cargo bed side rails. The seats can be folded down and stowed when not in use. Soldier-requested improvements have been incorporated into the A1 models, such as more ergonomic and stronger grab-bars for easier cab entry, increased protection against brush damage to a variety of external components, and reinforced rear light carriers. The FMTV series incorporates a new, more powerful engine that meets the more stringent United States Environment Protection Agency emissions standards and delivers up to a 22 percent increase in horsepower and up to a 28 percent increase in torque.

SPECIFICATIONS

Type:	medium truck
Manufacturer:	Stewart & Stevenson
Powerplant:	Caterpillar 6.6-litre diesel
Horsepower:	290
Transmission:	7-speed automatic
Length:	8.86m (29.06ft)
Width:	2.43m (7.97ft)
Height:	2.84m (9.31ft)
Weight:	9451kg (20,792lb)
Ground clearance:	0.55m (1.8ft)
Armament:	none
Crew:	1
Top speed:	94km/h (58.75mph)
Range:	645km (403 miles)
Fording:	0.91m (2.98ft)
Gradient:	60 percent
Configuration:	4 x 4

M1093

The FMTV brings state-of-the-art commercial truck technology to military tactical vehicles with an Anti-Lock Braking System on both the trucks and companion trailers, including an exhaust retarder, a Central Tire Inflation System (CTIS) for changing terrains, and an ultra high-speed J1939 electronic Databus. This Databus makes the new Interactive Electronic Technical Manual, or IETM, possible. This Class 5 IETM – the most advanced on the market – with intrusive diagnostics plugs into the central nervous system of the vehicle and interactively works with the vehicle's four separate electronic control units. Utilizing the highest resolution available, the IETM identifies vehicle problems and solutions, calls out necessary tools and hardware and provides detailed repair instructions – increasing overall efficiency and accuracy of maintenance tasks. The M1093 Standard Cargo Truck is designed to be loaded on and dropped from C-130 aircraft into remote areas where landing strips are not available. The vehicle is equipped to transport cargo and soldiers, as required. The M1093 has a payload capacity of 4545kg (10,000lb) and to facilitate loading/unloading of cargo, the bed side rails are mounted on hinges.

SPECIFICATIONS

Type:	cargo truck
Manufacturer:	Stewart & Stevenson
Powerplant:	Caterpillar 6.6-litre diesel
Horsepower:	290
Transmission:	7-speed automatic
Length:	6.93m (22.73ft)
Width:	2.43m (7.97ft)
Height:	2.84m (9.31ft)
Weight:	9498kg (20,896lb)
Ground clearance:	0.55m (1.8ft)
Armament:	none
Crew:	1
Top speed:	94km/h (58.75mph)
Range:	483km (302 miles)
Fording:	0.91m (2.98ft)
Gradient:	60 percent
Configuration:	6 x 6

MTVR

The US Marine Corps' Medium Tactical Vehicle Replacement (MTVR) offers a revolution in offroad mobility. With the Oshkosh Modular Independent Suspension (OMIS) system, the MTVR achieves levels of performance never before realized in a tactical wheeled vehicle, enabling the MTVR to traverse terrain previously regarded as impassable by trucks. The truck utilizes the latest in technological advancements, including IDS (independent suspension), auto-traction control and anti-lock braking systems. Long and short wheel base cargoes are currently in production, with dump, wrecker and other variants to be added. It can run with any ground-based military vehicle in US service, including M1 main battle tanks. The TAK-4 independent suspension system assures good handling, both on and off road, better traction, more upright stability, higher ground clearance and better suspension durability. In addition, it provides better overall vehicle durability because it filters out high frequency, low-amplitude vibrations that shake vehicle components loose. The MTVR can tow up to 10,000kg (22,000lb), such as a field howitzer or a full load of ammunition. It can also be transported by air in the fuselage of a C-130 Hercules transport aircraft or slung under a CH-53 helicopter.

SPECIFICATIONS

Type:	medium truck
Manufacturer:	Oshkosh
Powerplant:	Caterpillar C12
Horsepower:	425
Transmission:	7 + 1
Length:	8m (26.24ft)
Width:	2.48m (8.13ft)
Height:	3.58m (11.74ft)
Weight:	28,214kg (62,070lb)
Ground clearance:	0.42m (1.37ft)
Armament:	none
Crew:	1
Top speed:	105km/h (65.62mph)
Range:	483km (302 miles)
Fording:	1.5m (4.9ft)
Gradient:	60 percent
Configuration:	6 x 6

P114CB 6 X 6

Good overall operating economy is the result of a number of different factors, including purchase price and low running costs. This means low fuel consumption, good reliability, a long service life and simple maintenance – crucial to military operations. All Scania trucks are built on the basis of these requirements. Scania manufactures trucks for civilian and defence purposes, and is among the leaders when it comes to engineering, operational dependability and economy, a fact clearly borne out by the number of Scanias in military service around the world. Scania policy is to use standard commercial components also for defence applications. This has major advantages in terms of tailor-made specification, simplified part stockage training and servicing. As the company views it, an automotive manufacturer can derive decided advantages from developing and producing both civilian and defence trucks. For example, what is learnt on the civilian side can be turned to account when building defence vehicles and vice versa. The end result is Scania products displaying high performance, optimal economy and long service life. By drawing on a large number of standardized modules the company can build a large number of truck models and variants.

SPECIFICATIONS

Type:	heavy truck
Manufacturer:	Scania
Powerplant:	DC11 diesel
Horsepower:	340
Transmission:	automatic
Length:	7.3m (23.95ft)
Width:	2.43m (7.97ft)
Height:	3.3m (10.82ft)
Weight:	29,500kg (64,900lb)
Ground clearance:	0.4m (1.31ft)
Armament:	none
Crew:	1
Top speed:	105km/h (65.62mph)
Range:	600km (375 miles)
Fording:	0.8m (2.62ft)
Gradient:	40 percent
Configuration:	6 x 6

P124CB 6 X 6

his versatile truck is now in Swedish service. In February 2000 Scania signed an agreement with the Swedish Defence Materiel Administration for the supply of heavy trucks to the armed forces of that country. Up to 200 trucks will be delivered, and the Administration has an option to order additional trucks for delivery at a later date. The deal is the latest example of Scania being an important supplier to military customers. The vehicles, which are adapted for military duty, are fully based on Scania's civilian product concept. This gives access to the whole range of civilian parts and components, as well as Scania's service network. This has a positive effect, not least in terms of operating and maintenance costs. The majority of trucks are Scania P124 CB 6x6 with all-wheel-drive. The Multilift swap-body from HIAB Sverige AB will be fitted by Zetterbergs Produkt AB once the trucks have been delivered. Some of the trucks intended for international peacekeeping tasks have extra equipment such as additional protection for the cab, including mine shields. The P124 offers low running costs, low fuel consumption, good reliability, a long service life and simple maintenance. The truck in the picture is carrying two BV206 vehicles.

SPECIFICATIONS

Type:	hooklift
Manufacturer:	Scania
Powerplant:	DSC 12 diesel
Horsepower:	360
Transmission:	automatic
Length:	9.04m (29.65ft)
Width:	2.34m (7.67ft)
Height:	3.34m (10.95ft)
Weight:	28,000kg (61,600lb)
Ground clearance:	0.4m (1.31ft)
Armament:	none
Crew:	1
Top speed:	105km/h (65.62mph)
Range:	500km (312 miles)
Fording:	0.8m (2.62ft)
Gradient:	40 percent
Configuration:	6 x 6

P124CB 8 X 8

This is an an eight-wheel-drive off-road vehicle based on the company's modular system of standard components. The new truck had its premiere public showing at the leading military trade fair, Eurosatory in Paris, in 2000. The first customer to sign an order was FMV, the Swedish Defence Materiel Administration, which has placed an initial order for nine of the new trucks. They are part of a larger FMV order of just over 200 vehicles. The nine FMV trucks are all powered by the 420-horsepower Scania 12-litre engine. Although the first customer to sign an order was from the military, Scania's engineers see a variety of civilian application areas for a four-axle, all-wheel drive truck, for example as a tipper in particularly demanding operating conditions. In military guise, the emphasis is on robust resources for heavy off-road haulage duties. Scania's military vehicles are based on the company's civilian product range, which means that the entire civilian component range and parts-supply system is fully available, as well as Scania's global service network, which currently encompasses 1500 workshops in about 100 countries. This has a positive effect on operating and maintenance costs, and makes Scania's trucks attractive to potential customers, especially those in the developing world with limited budgets.

SPECIFICATIONS

Type:	off-road truck
Manufacturer:	Scania
Powerplant:	Scania Euro 2 diesel
Horsepower:	420
Transmission:	automatic
Length:	9.42m (30.9ft)
Width:	2.66m (8.72ft)
Height:	3.34m (10.95ft)
Weight:	34,000kg (74,800lb)
Ground clearance:	0.4m (1.31ft)
Armament:	none
Crew:	1
Top speed:	90km/h (56.25mph)
Range:	500km (312 miles)
Fording:	0.8m (2.62ft)
Gradient:	40 percent
Configuration:	8 x 8

PINZGAUER

The Pinzgauer range of all-terrain vehicles was developed by Steyr-Daimler-Puch as the successor to the Haflinger range of 4 x 4 vehicles. The 4 x 4 is available in two types of body: fully enclosed or with a military type body. The former has an all-steel, fully enclosed body with two doors each side and a single door at the rear. The military type body has a single door each side for the driver and one passenger. The tops of the doors can be removed, the windscreen folded down onto the bonnet, and the rear cargo area has removable bows and a tarpaulin cover. The chassis consists of a torsion resistant central tube with independent swing axles incorporating the transfer case and axle drive. The drive shaft is to the front and rear differentials are within the central tube chassis. This versatile vehicle can be fitted with optional equipment, including antenna holder, camouflage net holders, convoy lights, blackout blinds, divided windscreen, jerrycan holders, rear mounting trays, rifle holders, mounting points for shovels, rear tow hook and split battery system. A number in Austrian Army service have been fitted with 20mm anti-aircraft guns at the rear, with spare drum magazines stowed to the immediate rear of the driver's position. The Pinzgauer first entered military service, with Austria, in 1973.

SPECIFICATIONS

Type:	all-terrain vehicle
Manufacturer:	Steyr-Daimler-Puch
Powerplant:	Steyr air-cooled petrol
Horsepower:	87
Transmission:	5 + 1
Length:	4.17m (13.68ft)
Width:	1.76m (5.77ft)
Height:	2m (6.56ft)
Weight:	2100kg (4620lb)
Ground clearance:	0.33m (1.08ft)
Armament:	none
Crew:	1
Top speed:	110km/h (68.75mph)
Range:	600km (375 miles)
Fording:	0.7m (2.29ft)
Gradient:	80 percent
Configuration:	4 x 4

PLS

The Palletized Load System (PLS) is composed of a prime mover truck with integral self-loading and unloading transport capability, a trailer and demountable cargo beds (flatracks). The vehicle can also be equipped with materiel handling equipment and/or a winch. PLS is a key transportation component of the ammunition distribution system and can perform long-range hauling, local hauling and unit resupply of ammunition. The PLS tactical truck is a five-axle, 10-wheel drive vehicle equipped with a 500 horsepower Detroit Diesel engine, Allison automatic transmission and Central Tire Inflation System (CTIS). This combination provides a highly mobile system capable of transporting its payload in virtually any type of terrain, in any type of weather, and maintaining pace with the self-propelled artillery systems that it supports. The PLS comes in two mission oriented configurations: the M1074 and the M1075. The M1074 is equipped with a variable reach Material Handling Crane (MHC) to support forward deployed field artillery units. The M1075 is used in conjunction with the M1076 trailer but does not have the MHC. Ammunition can be loaded onto flatracks at depots, transported via container ship to theatre, picked up by the PLS truck and carried forward to line units.

SPECIFICATIONS

Type:	*heavy truck and trailer*
Manufacturer:	*Oshkosh*
Powerplant:	*Detroit Diesel Model 8V92TA*
Horsepower:	*500*
Transmission:	*5 + 1*
Length:	*10.67m (35ft)*
Width:	*2.43m (7.97ft)*
Height:	*3.28m (10.76ft)*
Weight:	*39,916kg (87,815lb)*
Ground clearance:	*unknown*
Armament:	*none*
Crew:	*1*
Top speed:	*91km/h (56.87mph)*
Range:	*1000km (625 miles)*
Fording:	*1.21m (3.97ft)*
Gradient:	*60 percent*
Configuration:	*10 x 10*

RB-44

This truck can be used for a variety of roles, such as troop carrier, towing a 105mm artillery piece or mounting an anti-tank missile system. The vehicle has a ladder-type bolted chassis which can accommodate various types of body. The cab is a standard three-seat type, but a conversion for carrying extra personnel and equipment is also available depending on mission requirements. The suspension system employs conventional semi-elliptical springs, fitted with double-acting telescopic shock absorbers. The brakes are vacuum-assisted with a dual-servo split system, and fitted front and rear. The front and rear axles have hypo gearing with a ratio of 4.1 to 1. The front axle's plated capacity is 2500kg (5500lb) and that of the rear 2800kg (6160lb). Variants of the vehicle include general service cargo body, soft and hard top bodies and an ambulance body. The front-mounted winch can be added to any version. The vehicle comes in three wheelbase lengths. The RB-44 was one of two final contenders for the British Army's 2-ton Truck Universal Heavy requirement, and was selected as the winner in mid-1988. The initial order was for 1000 vehicles, but the final figure was nearly double this. The RB-44 entered British Army service in 1989.

SPECIFICATIONS

Type:	*medium truck*
Manufacturer:	*Reynolds Boughton*
Powerplant:	*Perkins 110T diesel*
Horsepower:	*109*
Transmission:	*5 + 1*
Length:	*6.03m (19.78ft)*
Width:	*2.1m (6.88ft)*
Height:	*2.35m (7.7ft)*
Weight:	*5300kg (11,660lb)*
Ground clearance:	*0.3m (0.98ft)*
Armament:	*none*
Crew:	*1*
Top speed:	*109km/h (68.12mph)*
Range:	*500km (312 miles)*
Fording:	*0.75m (2.46ft)*
Gradient:	*33 percent*
Configuration:	*4 x 4*

T815-21

This truck is an offroad vehicle which has the ability to negotiate difficult terrain. Designed as a cargo or troop carrier, it has all-wheel drive and a front axle whose drive can be disconnected. In addition, it features axle and inter-axle differential locks and a central tyre inflation system. The truck has the TATRA suspension system. This features a rigid central "backbone" tube, with no torsion or bending of the chassis or superstructure. The result is a safe and trouble-free transport of sensitive loads, a high ride comfort, a faster drive offroad and a longer chassis life. All drive line shafts and other components are covered and protected inside the "backbone" tube, and each wheel moves up and down independently. This means that the vehicle can achieve higher speeds on rough roads, can traverse obstacles more easily, has excellent offroad mobility, and can absorb shocks and vibrations caused by rugged surfaces. Also, the swing half-axles are extremely resistant against impacts and shocks. TATRA has ensured a modular design for its axles, which means there is a high degree of commonality between its commercial and military models. The rear axle is sprung by the TATRA combination suspension airbags with coil springs inside, located above the central backbone.

SPECIFICATIONS

Type:	cargo truck
Manufacturer:	TATRA
Powerplant:	TATRA T3B-928
Horsepower:	450
Transmission:	10 + 2
Length:	6.88m (22.57ft)
Width:	2.6m (8.53ft)
Height:	2.99m (9.8ft)
Weight:	14,100kg (31,020lb)
Ground clearance:	0.36m (1.18ft)
Armament:	none
Crew:	1
Top speed:	120km/h (75mph)
Range:	1000km (625 miles)
Fording:	1.2m (3.93ft)
Gradient:	60 percent
Configuration:	4 x 4

T815-21VV25

TATRA produce all-round-drive vehicles with axle configurations of 4 x 4, 6 x 6, 8 x 8 and independent suspension of half-axles (TATRA chassis design concept). These vehicles provide excellent vibration attenuation and high operation speed on poor-quality roads. Tested in an extensive spectrum of operation conditions, provided with axle and inter-axle differential locks to go through the most adverse terrain, and with power trains protected against damage, these vehicles are rugged. They have a high-rigidity load-carrying structure, resulting in minimum longitudinal distortion, in contrast to traditional chassis found on other vehicles. Like all TATRA trucks, this vehicle has dual-circuit pressure air brakes acting on all wheels. The cab is all-metal with a curved windscreen and manhole in the roof. It is heated via a radiator supplied with engine oil. Gear change is pressure assisted by means of a gearshift lever with pre-selector for ease of operation. The cargo body has steel sideboards and a floor made of waterproof plywood covered with an anti-slip layer. The core of the truck is the chassis, and this design concept facilitates a simple distribution of forces from a trailer and/or additional equipment (such as a snow plough blade) onto the structure.

SPECIFICATIONS

Type:	cargo truck
Manufacturer:	TATRA
Powerplant:	TATRA T3B-928.10
Horsepower:	308
Transmission:	10 + 2
Length:	7.96m (26.11ft)
Width:	2.6m (8.53ft)
Height:	2.99m (9.8ft)
Weight:	26,000kg (57,200lb)
Ground clearance:	0.36m (1.18ft)
Armament:	none
Crew:	1
Top speed:	120km/h (75mph)
Range:	900km (563 miles)
Fording:	1.2m (3.93ft)
Gradient:	60 percent
Configuration:	6 x 6

T815-260R24

This is a special 6 x 6 medium mobility chassis with front-wheel drive disconnect, equipped with a Multilift Mk IV load-handling unit and capable of transporting flatracks or heavy containers loaded up to the maximum payload weight of 15,000kg (33,000lb). Equipped with a special adaptor "H-frame", it can handle European standardized containers. Standard equipment on the vehicle includes all-wheel drive with front axle drive disconnect, ABS, and cross and inter-axle differential locks. TATRA trucks are grouped into so-called "families" for ease of manufacture and standardization of parts. The ARMAX family is composed of trucks or chassis based on production commercial vehicles, which meet European emission, noise and axle load standards. The FORCE family are special trucks or chassis, both commercial and military, which use several different makes of water-cooled engines, special or automatic transmissions, and other high-performance design features enhancing the offroad mobility of the chassis. There is no doubt that the company's vehicles are well designed and proven: over 355,000 trucks and chassis using TATRA concepts have been produced since World War II. The range has been especially successful in Eastern Europe and in the former Soviet Union.

SPECIFICATIONS

Type:	*logistics truck*
Manufacturer:	*TATRA*
Powerplant:	*TATRA T3B-928.60*
Horsepower:	*340*
Transmission:	*10 + 2*
Length:	*8.35m (27.39ft)*
Width:	*2.5m (8.2ft)*
Height:	*3.14m (10.3ft)*
Weight:	*28,700kg (63,140lb)*
Ground clearance:	*0.31m (1.01ft)*
Armament:	*none*
Crew:	*1*
Top speed:	*95km/h (59.37mph)*
Range:	*600km (375 miles)*
Fording:	*1.2m (3.93ft)*
Gradient:	*69 percent*
Configuration:	*6 x 6*

T815-260R81

This vehicle is a special 8 x 8 mobility chassis with front-wheel drive disconnect and equipped with a Multilift Mk IV load-handling unit. The engine is air-cooled and supercharged with eight cylinders. The clutch is a single disc with a Belleville washer, and the gearbox is 10-speed mechanical, synchromeshed with a pneumatic gearshift booster and an electro-pneumatic engagement of normal or reduced drive mode. Brake units are equipped with automatic play adjustment. The TATRA chassis design idea is based on the time-proved idea of a backbone tube. No other truck can follow an uneven road profile in the same way as a TATRA truck. Excellent driving characteristics, especially in offroad environments, result from the special design of the chassis, first of all that of the sturdy backbone tube, consisting of the central load-carrying tube, independently suspended half-axles and cross-members. In comparison with a conventional-designed truck, this means a very rigid load-carrying structure, distinguished mainly by several times higher torsion strength and very high bend strength. A low torsion and bending load transferred to a superstructure enables the manufacturer to join it with the undercarriage in a simple manner. In addition, add-on equipment attachments are of simple design.

SPECIFICATIONS

Type:	*logistics truck*
Manufacturer:	*TATRA*
Powerplant:	*TATRA T3B-928.60*
Horsepower:	*340*
Transmission:	*10 + 2*
Length:	*8.68m (28.47ft)*
Width:	*2.5m (8.2ft)*
Height:	*4m (13.12ft)*
Weight:	*32,000kg (70,400lb)*
Ground clearance:	*0.3m (0.98ft)*
Armament:	*none*
Crew:	*1*
Top speed:	*90km/h (56.25mph)*
Range:	*650km (406 miles)*
Fording:	*1.2m (3.93ft)*
Gradient:	*63 percent*
Configuration:	*8 x 8*

T816-6MWV27

Thisis a platform truck that has been specifically designed to operate in temperature extremes. The TATRA T816 range has a 6 x 6 configuration with permanent drive of both rear axles and an option to switch to front axle drive if need be. The front axle suspension consists of torsion bars, while the rear axles have air bellows and spring coils. Engine choice is as follows: Cummins M11 ISM 400 water-cooled in-line six-cylinder (for 6 x 6 vehicles), Deutz water-cooled, eight-cylinder 400 kW (for 8 x 8 vehicles), or MTU water-cooled, 12-cylinder 610 kW (for 8 x 8 vehicles). Gearbox configuration is as follows: automatic, 6 speed plus 1 reverse or 10 speed plus 1 reverse (for 8 x 8 vehicles). The electronically controlled transmission is incorporated directly into the backbone tube and forms an integral part of the chassis structure. This design makes it possible for the transmission to work also as a transfer box, thus no transfer box is needed. The transmission has a number of useful features, including a so-called "limp-home" function and a shift-and-fault indicator. The cab is the all-metal type, with two cabin doors, a manhole in the roof, two full-size seats and an emergency seat located on the engine cover. The cabin tilt can be operated either manually or hydraulically.

SPECIFICATIONS

Type:	*cargo truck*
Manufacturer:	*TATRA*
Powerplant:	*Cummins ISM 400*
Horsepower:	*400*
Transmission:	*6 + 1*
Length:	*9.06m (29.72ft)*
Width:	*2.55m (8.36ft)*
Height:	*3.55m (11.64ft)*
Weight:	*26,000kg (57,200lb)*
Ground clearance:	*0.36m (1.18ft)*
Armament:	*none*
Crew:	*1*
Top speed:	*104km/h (65mph)*
Range:	*600km (375 miles)*
Fording:	*1.2m (3.93ft)*
Gradient:	*60 percent*
Configuration:	*6 x 6*

T816-6VWN9T

This semi-trailer prime mover is designed to haul semi-trailers transporting tanks, armoured personnel carriers and other heavy vehicles up to a maximum weight of 74,000kg (162,800lb) both on roads and on rugged terrain. The prime mover is also designed to operate in temperature extremes, high air humidity and in dusty environments (air conditioning is an option for the cab but is not fitted as standard). The fully automatic electronically controlled 10-speed transmission has hydraulic power shift, integral torque biasing lockable inter-axle differential, limp-home function and fault indicator. The front and rear axles have independent suspension sprung by leaf springs and telescopic shock absorbers. The powerful engine is the MTU 12V 183 TD22, which is a water-cooled, four-stroke, turbocharged and charge-air-cooled direct injection diesel unit. The vehicle has left-hand power-assisted steering, and is fitted with two winches that have cables with operating lengths of 70m (230ft) each. An auxiliary winch has an operating length of 150m (492ft). The brake system comprises wedge-type self-adjusting brake units, while the emergency brake is a spring type that acts on the wheels of the rear axles.

SPECIFICATIONS

Type:	prime mover
Manufacturer:	TATRA
Powerplant:	MTU 12V 183 TD22
Horsepower:	800
Transmission:	10 + 2
Length:	9.02m (29.59ft)
Width:	2.78m (9.02ft)
Height:	3.51m (11.51ft)
Weight:	43,800kg (96,360lb)
Ground clearance:	0.4m (1.31ft)
Armament:	none
Crew:	1
Top speed:	85km/h (53.12mph)
Range:	1000km (625 miles)
Fording:	1.25m (4.1ft)
Gradient:	32 percent
Configuration:	8 x 8

T816 8 X 8

The T816 forms the backbone of a whole family of military vehicles produced by TATRA. The example shown above is the logistics truck. Other vehicles in the range include a fuel tanker, which has four independent drums and hoses that make it possible to refuel four vehicles at once via fast-clip high-pressure tails or fast-clip filling guns. The water tanker version has a stainless steel tank designed for the transport of drinking water for front-line troops with baffles and bulkheads inside. The engine common to all variants is a water-cooled, four-stroke tur-bocharged model with direct diesel injection. The transmission is electronically controlled, fully automatic and is integrated into the chassis backbone tube. The vehicle has a limp-home function and shift-and-fault indicator. A crane is mounted on the rear of the logistics truck, which has a maximum horizontal capacity of 1000kg (2200lb) and a maximum load capacity of 2945kg (6479lb). Manually tiltable, it has hydraulically extendable supporting legs. The cab is of all-metal construction with two doors, flat split roof and manhole in the roof. The cargo body has a steel frame, aluminium side boards and a floor made of water-resistant plywood with an anti-slip surface.

SPECIFICATIONS

Type:	logistics truck
Manufacturer:	TATRA
Powerplant:	Deutz BF8M 1015C diesel
Horsepower:	536
Transmission:	6 + 1
Length:	9.37m (30.74ft)
Width:	2.6m (8.53ft)
Height:	3.19m (10.46ft)
Weight:	30,800kg (67,760lb)
Ground clearance:	0.41m (1.34ft)
Armament:	none
Crew:	1
Top speed:	120km/h (75mph)
Range:	1000km (625 miles)
Fording:	1.25m (4.1ft)
Gradient:	37 percent
Configuration:	8 x 8

UNIMOG

The Unimog has a long history, being designed in 1946 and first produced in 1948. Though there are a number of variants in the range, all vehicles have the same basic layout with the engine and cab at the front and the cargo area at the rear. Most of the military variants have a two-door cab with a hard or soft top and a windscreen that folds down onto the bonnet. The cargo area has a drop tailgate, drop sides, removable bows and a tarpaulin cover. All Unimogs have excellent cross-country performance, being fitted with four-wheel drive and differential locks on both the front and rear axles. On roads it is usual for only the rear wheels to be engaged, while on rough terrain all wheels are engaged. In use with nearly 40 countries worldwide, Unimogs are used in a variety of roles, including ambulance, command vehicle, firefighting vehicle, radio vehicle, workshop and prime mover for artillery pieces up to 105mm in calibre. Options include a fully enclosed cab, generator, snow ploughs and winch. Mercedes-Benz are constantly updating the Unimog with different transmissions and powerplants. Essentially, however, the shell of the vehicle is much the same as it was when it rolled off the production line only three years after the end of World War II.

SPECIFICATIONS

Type:	light truck
Manufacturer:	Mercedes-Benz
Powerplant:	OM 352 diesel
Horsepower:	536
Transmission:	4 + 4
Length:	5.54m (18.17ft)
Width:	2.3m (7.54ft)
Height:	2.7m (8.85ft)
Weight:	5250kg (11,550lb)
Ground clearance:	0.44m (1.44ft)
Armament:	none
Crew:	1
Top speed:	82km/h (51.25mph)
Range:	700km (437 miles)
Fording:	1.2m (3.93ft)
Gradient:	70 percent
Configuration:	4 x 4

INDEX

Picture Credits

Alvis Vehicles Limited: 38, 41, 42
Aviation Photographs International: 34, 81, 101, 102, 118, 178, 188
BAe Systems: 31
Bofors Defence: 143
Caterpillar: 130, 131
Crown Copyright: 33, 36, 37, 39, 40, 43, 100, 103, 104, 107, 124, 127, 128, 129, 132, 137, 138, 146, 153, 154, 156, 159, 160, 161,180
General Dynamics: 95, 109
Grove: 120
Hägglunds Moelv AS: 12, 122, 123, 142, 155
Iveco S.p.A.: 48, 49, 99, 119, 149, 152, 162, 163, 164, 165
KMW: 21, 22, 24, 26, 28, 29, 74
Lockheed Martin: 11
MAN Technologie AG: 105
Mowag: 112, 113, 114, 115, 133
Oshkosh Truck Corporation: 148, 158, 174, 179
Patria Vehicles: 116, 144
Private collection: 56
Rheinmetall Landsysteme GmbH: 106, 125, 126, 139, 145
Scania: 150, 175, 176, 177
Stewart & Stevenson Tactical Vehicle Systems: 170, 171, 172, 173
TATRA: 151, 181, 182, 183, 184, 185, 186, 187
Tim Ripley: 15, 46, 51, 58, 59, 67, 71, 72, 73, 85, 89, 93
The Tank Museum, Bovington: 8, 9, 13, 20, 25, 47, 50, 54, 61, 64, 66, 68, 69, 92, 97
TRAK International: 117
TRH Pictures: 14, 16, 18, 19, 23, 27, 30, 44, 52, 53, 55, 57, 60, 62, 63, 70, 82
US DoD: 10, 17, 32, 35, 45, 65, 75, 76, 77, 78, 79, 80, 83, 84, 86, 87, 88, 90, 91, 93, 96, 108, 111, 121, 134, 135, 136, 140, 141, 166, 167, 168, 169
Volvo: 147, 157